The Man Behind the Bow Tie

ARTHUR PORTER
with *T.R. TODD*

The

MAN

Behind the

BOW

Tie

ARTHUR PORTER ON BUSINESS,
POLITICS AND INTRIGUE

Figure.1
Vancouver / Berkeley

Cataloguing data available from Library and Archives Canada
ISBN 978-1-927958-12-4 (cloth)
ISBN 978-1-927958-13-1 (ebook)

Editing by Barbara Berson
Copy editing by Peter Norman
Jacket and interior design by Jessica Sullivan
Jacket photograph by dra_schwartz, iStock Photo
Printed and bound in Canada by Friesens
Distributed in the U.S. by Publishers Group West

Figure 1 Publishing Inc.
Vancouver BC Canada
www.figure1pub.com

For my family.

I dedicate this book to my father and mother, who created me, nurtured me and gave me the spirit to overcome and succeed. I also dedicate this book to my wife, Pamela, and my daughters, Gemma, Fiona, Adina and Charlotte— "Team Porter," who supported me through geography, time, success and adversity.

I am truly in your debt. This may be my story, but it's for you.

CONTENTS

PREFACE

IN MY JAIL cell in Panama, I have a bed, a lamp and a fan. A thin curtain separates me from the nine other prisoners sharing this cell. Beyond, hundreds of hardened criminals are roaming the halls. I have swelling around my ankles and shortness of breath. When I put my stethoscope to my chest, I hear more crackles than before. I have an idea of what a chest x-ray would show, and it's not good. I occasionally cough blood, but overall, thanks to drugs I smuggled into prison, I am functioning well for a fifty-seven-year-old man with lung cancer, who hasn't seen a doctor in months.

Sitting here, I think about the world beyond these walls. I think about my wife, who is under house arrest in Montreal, and my four daughters, spread out across the globe. I think about the charges against me in Canada. Fraud. Conspiracy to commit fraud. Fraud against the government. I think about the damage to my reputation and the fair-weather friends who have come and gone. And I think about the next meeting with my lawyer and how I will get out of this place.

It is a lot to take in, and it is not always easy to keep a brave face. But there are many ways to get through it. One way is to view my cancer dispassionately, as something outside myself. I notice improvements or setbacks and move on.

Another way is to stay as busy and productive as I can. I never sit still. I solve problems and perform tasks. I improve my living quarters. I go for walks and conduct business. Or I treat patients, my fellow inmates, for injuries, infections and diseases. I focus on the next goal. That is how I survive.

Days like today are especially difficult. After all, it was two years ago today that my life started to unravel.

WHEN THE MEDIA has turned their attention to me, whether in glowing or disparaging articles in the newspaper or on the nightly news, they always seem to be fascinated with just how a half-black, half-white boy from Africa got to where he was. Perhaps because I've never stayed in one place for too long, or because I'm always making new friends and pursuing new business partnerships, or maybe it's as simple as my being neither black nor white—for whatever reason, people have always had difficulty pinning me down or slotting me into a category. Some have considered me chameleon-like, changing colours to suit my environment.

It's true: I have lived and worked in Sierra Leone, England, Canada, the United States, the Caribbean and everywhere in between. But that is where the comparison ends. Unlike a chameleon, I have never blended into my environment—ever. Nor have I wanted to do so. I got people to adapt to suit me, regardless of race, religion or social position. I reshaped the environment to the way I wanted it. I made other people's colours change.

Recently, a good friend of mine died. Winston Derrick was the former editor of the *Antigua Observer*. He was a gregarious man, full of jokes, argument and wit, and always with a twinkle in his eye. While having dinner with a friend at a restaurant, he succumbed to a massive pulmonary embolism, a blockage to the main artery in the lung that caused a near-instant death.

I was not there at the time, but the image of Winston sprawled on a restaurant floor, amid panic and confusion, has stuck in my mind. He had no time to think about or plan his departure from this earth. He did not get to say goodbye to whomever he wished or to deal with his affairs. He believed he was in perfect health.

I know better. I have terminal lung cancer, and I am fighting to stay alive in an environment far from ideal for my (or anyone's) health and well-being. My entire life has been devoted to climbing, winning and succeeding. But with the end drawing near, it is inevitable that I, like anyone else, wonder if what I have accomplished truly matters. I wonder how I will be remembered. Unlike Winston, I have this moment to consider these questions.

If my situation has a silver lining, I think it is this: my illness has prioritized what is important. And so I have decided to tell my own story, in my own words, about how a Sierra Leonean reached the highest offices in Canada and the U.S. I challenge my critics to keep an open mind. Amid all the controversies and allegations, there is another side to this story. There is an African boy with a heart, a mind and a desire to succeed—a human being. Now we can all look back and see more clearly how Arthur Porter—doctor, businessman, statesman, spy watchdog, husband and father— went from the halls of power to the hell of La Joya.

Whether the journey is worthy of remembrance, I leave to you, the reader.

NOVEMBER 8, 2013
La Joya Prison, Panama

1.

FROM A
GREAT HEIGHT

I STEPPED OUT of the London taxi with my head spinning, my BlackBerry clutched in my shaky palm. Before me was 20 Moorgate, the Bank of England. I stood dwarfed by those towering columns, contemplating my next move.

On a typical day, a high-profile luncheon with Mark Carney, then governor of the Bank of Canada, would have been right up my alley. I relished nothing more than a networking opportunity. In the course of my life, my God-given predispositions have made me among the best at what I do. I have a strategic memory. In a sea full of ties and tuxedos, I always know exactly who is worth knowing. I am focused and charismatic. I take no prisoners. I have often heard it said that it is better to know the king than to be the king. Well, in my time I have known more than a few kings.

On November 8, 2011, I was at the height of my power. I had reached the pinnacle of my profession as a radiation oncologist. I served on dozens of prestigious political and scientific boards and committees. When I wasn't travelling,

I spent my weekdays in Montreal and weekends at my home in the Bahamas. Heads of state were my colleagues and friends. My international business dealings stretched across several continents, from North America to Africa, with interests in mining, real estate, infrastructure and health-care. I was a known Republican in the U.S., an avid Conservative in Canada and a man of influence in my native Sierra Leone. As a diplomat or an ambassador-at-large for Sierra Leone, I kept a party card in my wallet. I am member number 4,900 of the All People's Congress, which I joined in my home country some thirty-five years ago.

In Canada I was best known as director general and chief executive officer of the McGill University Health Centre. Under my leadership, we were finally building what people had dreamt about for nearly two decades—a new $1.3-billion mega-hospital in Montreal. I was also just months away from finishing my first term as chairman of the Security Intelligence Review Committee of Canada (SIRC), the watchdog for the Canadian Security Intelligence Service (CSIS). That was what had brought me to London: I was leading a Canadian delegation to meet our counterparts at MI5, the U.K.'s domestic counter-intelligence and security agency, something we did at least once a year.

In intelligence circles, there is a group known as the "five eyes," made up of mostly Commonwealth countries, including Britain, Canada, South Africa and Australia, as well as the U.S. On this particular day, however, all eyes were apparently on me, and not in a good way. En route to lunch, I had received an email from my public relations assistant at the McGill University Health Centre, alerting me to an article splashed across the front of one of Canada's daily newspapers. On any given day, I usually received a minimum of three hundred emails. I divided this correspondence into three groups. About a hundred of these emails fell into the CYA ("cover your ass") category: things subordinates and colleagues wanted to be sure they told me. Another hundred emails were useless, and those I ignored. The final hundred tended to be quite important.

The email I had just received was very important. It contained information that was serious, on the cusp of earthshattering. I knew that immediately from the subject line, written entirely in caps so I would not miss it: "ALERT: ARTICLE THIS MORNING IN NATIONAL POST." A horrible feeling festered in the pit of my stomach, hard and big, and I could feel it jamming itself up my throat. I coughed and shifted uncomfortably in the cab's black leather seat as I waited for the article to load.

The yellow banner of the *Post* flashed up, and I saw my picture and the headline. In truth, it was an expletive-worthy moment. One of Canada's largest newspapers had dredged up a botched deal I had attempted to broker more than a year earlier. The deal was between a Montreal-based businessman named Ari Ben-Menashe, the Sierra Leone government and myself.

Ben-Menashe was born in Iran and apparently worked for a time with Israeli intelligence. He was reported to have been involved in the trafficking of military equipment. He was also a well-known Russian lobbyist, though he worked with many other countries as well. A Canadian citizen, he owned a registered Canadian company, Traeger Resources and Logistics Inc. At the time he first approached me, I didn't know him well. I did know that he had sold military aircraft and other weaponry to various countries. Most people find those kinds of transactions quite frightful.

Contrary to popular belief, however, such deals are not terribly unusual. The Canadians do it. The Americans do it. While Ben-Menashe may have had a colourful past, I found it interesting that he was later portrayed as if he was an Al-Qaeda operative living in a cave on the Pakistani-Afghani border. In actuality, the man lived in Westmount, one of the most respectable areas of Montreal.

What Ben-Menashe had proposed to me a year earlier had nothing to do with weapons, but instead involved bridges, dams, ferries and other infrastructure projects in Sierra Leone. The Russians wanted to do this type of deal in Sierra Leone through a development organization. Russia was peddling influence, with the idea that the investments they made would be leveraged politically down the road. They were doing this in several parts of the world. In the case of Sierra Leone, the deal would have provided $150 million for the country. The arrangement would certainly have made the lives of Sierra Leoneans better.

Of course, others would have benefited as well. I was chairman of Africa Infrastructure Group, the company set to handle the project in Sierra Leone. The ruling government there also saw the deal as election fodder. They knew that dispersing millions of dollars throughout the country would endear them to the population. I had no idea what Ben-Menashe stood to gain. I did not ask, and he would not have told me. If you are brokering deals between Russians and West Africans, you don't want to ask too many questions about the players. Otherwise you will find it very difficult doing business in that part of the world.

I don't think many people understand the dynamics of international business. I had no illusions. Most business deals, if they are successful, have two sides to the story. All you can do is focus on your side. But the *National Post* article framed my actions as if they constituted a conflict of interest. According to the *Post*, by working with Ben-Menashe and foreign governments, I was being disloyal to Canada.

The deal fell apart in late December 2010. Ben-Menashe had assured me that he had the money and the project could move ahead. But then nothing happened. We had several conversations about the money he had promised. He told me it was in Paris, and later Rome. Around Christmastime I had a serious discussion with Ben-Menashe. I needed a definitive answer, since Ernest Bai Koroma, the president of Sierra Leone as well as my friend, was beginning to ask questions. If the deal was going bad, I wanted to rip off the Band-Aid and be done with it. So I asked Ben-Menashe straight out: Is the money coming? Over time, I grew tired of his assurances. I decided to pull the plug.

As I polished off the article, my mind was flashing between past and present. Meanwhile, our taxi had pulled up to the Bank of England and my colleagues were already getting out. They looked back inquisitively, but I told them to go ahead, waving and forcing a smile, my eyes still glued to the screen. This article, as horrible as it was, could not be ignored. I would have to respond, and quickly.

THE MORNING HAD started off normally. I was staying at the Marylebone Hotel on Welbeck Street. I always stayed there when in London. Hotels are like political parties. Once you stay at one several times in a row, it becomes more like a club. Loyalty breeds consistency, and I find that you are typically rewarded for your loyalty in the end. I have met people who believe that you can play on both sides of the fence. But it never works. True, there will always be a period when you are in the wilderness. But if you choose wisely, over time a clearing will present itself. People remember that, especially when it comes to business. In reality, everything I did was political. Any decision I made began with weighing up the political factions. You can change countries, but never your political stripes. As for hotels, I was far too absorbed in my professional life to leave anything to chance. I wanted quality and efficiency. I needed the carpet rolled out at my feet.

As I emerged from the lobby that morning, a bellhop greeted me by name with a bow and opened the door to the shuttle that had been arranged by the Canadian embassy. Before our delegation's meeting with MI5 and the luncheon at the Bank of England, I was scheduled to meet with Gordon Campbell, former premier of British Columbia and now Canada's ambassador to the U.K. With a Canadian delegation in town, it was expected that I meet with Campbell. It was a breakfast meeting, although in situations like these, you don't really have breakfast. The saucers, knives and forks, grilled kippers and toast were stage-play between actors. They were props for getting down to business.

A few other members of the Canadian delegation joined us. Campbell and I spoke about the security needs of the Canadian embassy in London, and the upcoming meeting planned for later that morning with officials from the Joint Intelligence Committee in central London.

People often have a skewed or even a sinister notion of the meetings between intelligence services. The participants don't sit in dark rooms with scattered spotlights, whispering and plotting the direction of the world. In a sense, these meetings are quite perfunctory. You do not share a lot of information in most cases, though you pretend to. The Americans claim that they share, but they don't, really. The same goes for Israel. Most agencies do their own thing and share only when it is practical or convenient. It is a cross between a chess match and diplomacy. In basic terms, by communicating regularly, each side feels comfortable asking for favours when the need arises. Intelligence is never a public show. The real information does not come from these meetings but from the operatives themselves or those working in the field. We sit around the table, all smiling and feeling good about ourselves but not expecting to do a lot of work.

That morning we stuck to safe topics, including Omar Khadr. Khadr was a Canadian citizen who had been captured by American forces in Afghanistan in connection with terrorist activities and suspected links to Al-Qaeda. Only fifteen when he was arrested, the child soldier became one of the youngest captives and the last Western citizen to be held in Guantanamo Bay, Cuba. Khadr was also the first person since the Second World War to be prosecuted in a military commission for war crimes committed while still a minor. Human rights groups and the media strongly criticized his eight-year prison sentence, especially after Canada did not seek extradition or repatriation.

The group also talked about other problems that faced us mutually, many of which involved operations in the Middle East and Afghanistan. How we handled prisoners was also on the table, with interrogation techniques a hot topic. We were always getting lambasted on the grounds of civil rights: whether it was fair to have a prisoner with one foot in a bucket of water and holding an electric bulb while asking him how cold it gets during winter in Canada. I am being facetious, of course. Canadians rarely got their hands dirty in a direct way. Nevertheless, questions about prisoners of war and interrogation techniques were daily realities I had to face during my tenure at SIRC. I will have plenty more to say on that later, dear reader.

NOW, OUTSIDE THE Bank of England, that morning meeting seemed distant. Attending the luncheon, at which Carney was delivering a speech to the British financial authorities, was the last thing I felt like doing. All I could think about was getting to a place where I could make phones calls and handle the scandal. My mind was calculating, measuring and planning. But my body was on autopilot. I straightened my blue bow tie, put on a smile and passed beneath the bank's imposing archway. I motored through the luncheon as if I was on a speed circuit. I stayed only long enough for people to know that I was there, and then strode crisply to the exit.

The cab raced me back to the Marylebone Hotel. When I got to the room, I poured myself a drink, then undid my tie and let it hang there around my neck. I never react on the spur of the moment, since you generally get it wrong. Although I reported directly to Stephen Harper, the prime minister of Canada, I was not going to call him and ask him to check out page one. I needed my people to speak with his people and take it up through the right security channels.

I spoke with Harper later that afternoon. The prime minister rarely displays too much emotion. I could have sat on it, and seen if the story had legs. I then spoke with Harper's chief of staff, who promised to get back to me about damage control. It was still too soon to tell whether there would be any serious ramifications in Ottawa. But I had already decided that I would resign my post as chairman of SIRC.

I could have flown to Ottawa and played the political game. I imagine Harper's communications team and I could have sat down and worked through every possible question the prime minister might face from the Liberals and New Democratic Party. But even if I got to stay, my reputation would be tarnished. The slightest hint of impropriety can be difficult to get rid of. It's like a splatter of ink on a white shirt lapel. No matter how much you scrub, people will still see a mark. I had lost the moral authority to fulfill my role at SIRC effectively. More importantly, I felt a genuine sense of loyalty towards Harper and the Conservative Party. I would have forced the prime minister to go through a challenging time during Question Period. I resigned the next day, just before he went into Parliament.

It didn't pay me anything to fall on my sword, except that it did buy the respect of some people who mattered. I did not want to hammer the Conservative Party, and because of that, Mr. Harper and I remained friends. I believe he wanted me to stay on. I think most people in the know felt I was doing a damn good job. An infrastructure deal that had never happened was not worth losing my job over. But truth be told, I had planned to resign shortly. My first term was ending, and approval for the $1.3-billion hospital in Montreal had come to fruition. With that mission accomplished, I intended to leave Canada and spend my days in the Bahamas, where I had a home and several businesses. I also wanted to head back to Sierra Leone on occasion. It was clear that one could not hold the SIRC chairmanship while living outside of Canada. Indeed, if I had decided to battle on and then resigned a short time later, I would not have endeared myself to Mr. Harper and the party.

So it was not a difficult decision to resign. There are really no tough decisions in life. When you look at all the factors and the evidence, your decision becomes easy.

Following my resignation, I called Ernest Bai Koroma to explain the situation. I followed up my call with a letter. The president was very much on my side, but he'd been unaware of the article. He had enough to worry about himself from Sierra Leone's thirteen or so newspapers.

President Koroma wasn't the only one with plenty to worry about.

I did not know it at the time, but that dreary day in London would change my life forever. Ben-Menashe was not my undoing, but looking back, it was the beginning of the end. The *National Post* story sparked a mudslide of accusations. There would be more articles, more urgent emails from my assistant in Montreal and more phone calls to my friends, allies and enemies. All of my appointments and accomplishments, my position and my prestige were about to implode.

I CARRIED ON in London for a few more days. I went to a couple of plays, ate at pleasant restaurants and drank some good wine. Most of the time, however, I worked, because I had a number of other business reasons to be in London. One of the reasons I love London is its conduciveness to international commerce. In the afternoon you can make calls to the U.S., and in the morning you can reach people in Asia. You are right on the timeline, and the city is roughly equidistant from North America and Singapore. While the weather may be terrible at times, London is the ideal business centre.

I did not have a lot of interests outside of work, in fact. I occasionally tried my hand at fishing, but after a while I got bored. It involved too much waiting. I wanted to negotiate with the fish: You bite the hook and flop in the boat, and we will take a picture and be done with it. That approach would be much easier.

For me, deal making and networking were truly orgasmic. I made the fish come to me. I loved getting people in a room to look at something from a completely new angle. I created energy between people by telling them what to do, without them realizing it, and they felt good about it.

I was always as strict with others as I was with myself. If I said I was going to do something, I did it, and I expected the same of others. But I never made anyone feel useless or stupid. In fact, I went out of my way to make people think they were smart, even smarter than me. People seem to like that. A slight correction: it gets you a long way with men, but in serious trouble with women.

Looking back, the deal with Ben-Menashe exposed one of my greatest shortcomings: I have never met a deal I did not like. The challenge was in making it work, and I enjoyed the buzz of wrangling and negotiation. As a result, I sometimes saw more capacity for a deal than was actually there. Throughout my life, I kept trying to do more, run faster and jump higher. When I was a boy, my mother used to tell me: "Arthur, you are trying to grow up too fast. You don't have to accomplish everything now. There is time."

My work with Ben-Menashe was not sordid or illegal in any way. I don't believe it was a conflict of interest and I would not have done anything differently. Deals will go bad, but if you don't try, you'll never make it. Sometimes when you fish, you reel in a glistening blue marlin. Other times, you come up with a dirty brown boot.

In my life, for the most part I've caught the big fish.

But mother was right. Perhaps I did move too quickly. It just caught up with me that day. In Greek mythology, Icarus, the son of a master craftsman, flew too close to the sun using wings fashioned from feathers and wax. Perhaps the sun was so bright and enticing, the sensation of flying so liberating, that Icarus could not help himself from climbing higher and higher. As for me, I just wanted to see how high I could fly.

In school, my teachers used to accuse me of having a chronic lack of focus. I could see big pictures, the grandiose plan spread out before my feet. We might be on step two, but in my mind, I was already on step ten. That kind of vision came at a price. Details were given short shrift. Sometimes I did not properly see or anticipate the perspective others had. I was always thinking about the next hill to climb.

At many points, I could have stopped my career from advancing and been successful as a doctor, a businessman or even a politician. But I kept searching for the next hill. Sometimes, it turned out that the hill beyond the hill was not a hill at all. It was a mountain, and too high for me to fly over without my wings melting.

But first, let me take you back to the beginning. I want to tell you about a young boy in Sierra Leone, whose wings were only just starting to grow.

2.

"ARTHUR, YOU WILL BE A DOCTOR"

ONE OF MY most vivid childhood memories is of my father calling my sister and me into his study on a rainy Sunday evening. It must have been the summer, perhaps May or June, because I remember it had rained for a week straight. A deluge like that was not unusual in Sierra Leone during the rainy season. The rain never stops and the temperature stays hot and sticky. I used to walk to school in my bathing suit; otherwise my school uniform—shirt, tie, shoes and slacks—would get drenched. It was a great way to bypass the shower. You could not wear a raincoat, either, because it was too hot. I was not the only one. Every morning, I saw droves of boys and girls, some gleeful and others melancholy, wearing bathing suits, with their school uniforms stuffed in plastic bags or already at school, waiting for them. During those months, nothing ever seemed to dry.

My father's study was his refuge. Dr. Arthur T. Porter III was a well-known Creole historian, lawyer and anthropologist in Sierra Leone, and indeed West Africa at large. At

Fourah Bay College in Freetown, the oldest university in the country, Professor Porter became somewhat of a legend and an authority in his field. He established the Department of African Studies at the university and wrote a number of books on West African history over the decades.

Education was our focus and priority in those early years. Most of my memories before the age of sixteen revolve around teachers and my studies. My father set high and clear expectations from the start. But being called into his study was unusual. My father was always busy reading, studying or out at the university.

My mother, who was of Danish origin, had met my father at Cambridge while she was studying to be a nurse. In our family, she was the ever-present disciplinarian, and she ran the household. So if my father got involved in the daily running of the house, it often meant that I had done something bad. Bad enough for him to stop whatever else he was doing. It sent my mind racing.

Wind and rain were lashing the windowpane as my sister and I stepped gingerly into the study. My father was reading at his desk in a dim light, as he often did. The walls were covered in books and historical anthologies. The tomes seemed like hundreds of bricks propping up the room.

My father rose from his desk, picked up two chairs and placed them before us. The three of us sat down to the collective creaking of old wood. He crossed his legs and ran one hand through his moustache.

"Arthur. Emma. The only careers I truly rate are the professions of doctor and lawyer," he said. "It's time to decide what you each want to be."

We had both known this conversation was coming. I was still a boy, and my sister was two years younger. But there had never been any question we would fall into one of these professions. My father let the statement hang there and fill the room.

He pointed at my sister. "Emma, what do you want to be?"

She looked at me and then at my father. "I want to be a lawyer."

My father smiled and nodded his head. "Arthur," he said, leaning forward in his chair, "you will be a doctor."

In that instant, our future was decided. I think my father had asked my sister first for a couple of reasons. First, she was the youngest. Second, my father knew I could do many things: medicine, accounting, business. I would take what was left. Either way, my sister and I chose wisely. We went on to excel in our selected fields. I became a noted and widely published oncologist, and my sister served as a senior lawyer for Canada's Department of Justice. My father's only fear was that I would become a politician. That is perhaps the reason I resisted doing that throughout my professional life. He felt that all politicians were crooks, liars and cheats. I suppose many of them are, but I always told him that you could not complain about the system if capable individuals failed to get involved in the political process. Nonetheless, my words failed to sway him.

AS ARTHUR PORTER IV, born in Freetown in 1956, I had very specific expectations placed upon me. At the same time, I had the sense that the world was at my feet. Our rich family history set the tone for this way of thinking. I am the descendant of freed slaves. In the early nineteenth century, slavery was abolished in many parts of the world, including the U.K. and its colonies. Arthur Porter I came to Freetown from the U.K. We do not know too much about him, except that he was a free man of Maroon extraction in Jamaica. Records from Manchester, England, dating back to 1803, identify him as a Freemason. At eighteen, I too was initiated into Freemasonry, and I have been an active member since then. I later became a Shriner and a Freemason to the thirty-second degree.

Arthur Porter I married a woman who had arrived in Sierra Leone from Nova Scotia. As I understand it, she was a freed slave who escaped from the U.S. through the Underground Railway, as so many did. She came through Detroit into Canada and ended up in Dresden, Ontario. The town was home to a black settlement and technical school founded by the famous Josiah Henson, the minister and abolitionist who is also believed to be the inspiration for George Harris, the fugitive slave in *Uncle Tom's Cabin*. Dresden had infrastructure, such as a mill and a sawmill. The idea was to provide hundreds of freed slaves with practical skills and the means to be self-sufficient. My great-great-great-grandmother lived there for a number of years, until the British decided that having ex-slaves in the wheat basket was not the best use of the land. She and her family were uprooted to Nova Scotia, where they helped set up another town, later known as Africville, near the Bedford Basin in Halifax.

Africville was the first black colony in Nova Scotia, and the people did not do particularly well there. It began as small and poor, largely cut off from the neighbouring society. Africville was destroyed in the 1960s to make way for the construction of the A. Murray MacKay Bridge. Shortly after its demolition and the forced relocation of its residents, the government apologized and rebuilt parts of the community. Canada designated Africville a National Historic Site in 1996. It remains emblematic of my ancestry and the long struggle against racism.

My great-great-great-grandmother, for her part, did not stay on in Canada. The Canadian government offered black people yet another deal. This time, they wanted to ship part of the population back to Africa. Her parents did not make the trip. They were buried in Nova Scotia. It must have been difficult for a young woman, presumably travelling alone, to embark on such a life-changing journey. I can only imagine how it would have felt to be one of the many people boarding three boats for the long voyage to the British colony known as Freetown. Historical records contain many interesting passages describing how these repatriated Africans sailed past slave boats on their way to the New World.

These boats, headed in two very different directions, represented the great changes beginning to occur in West African society. Like many others, my ancestors had been living outside of Africa for three generations or so. It was only natural that these people did not consider themselves Africans in the strictest sense of the word. They had lived as free men and women, received education and started businesses in North America. In Freetown, they went to church on Sundays. The men became Freemasons and wore top hats. If you look at a Sierra Leone phone book today, you will find some very Western names. The main language was English, but my ancestors spoke a form of Creole. Arthur Porter I met my great-great-great grandmother; they married and later established Porter's Royal Hotel. The building no longer exists, though I still have a decanter from the property.

The early Porters were people with means. Arthur Porter I was a landowner. He was also the consul to what was then the Belgian Congo. I'm quite sure he was involved in the slave trade in some capacity, since the industry was commonplace throughout Africa at this time. They would have called it indentured labouring.

My ancestors, having come from abroad, were considered fairly well-to-do. For the most part, this group did not mix well with the Africans. The social divide was clear and palpable. In addition to Western names, customs, dress and sensibilities, the members of this group aspired to be doctors and lawyers. Every family wanted that for their children, and certainly this sentiment was alive and well for my father, Arthur Porter III.

My father wrote often about this emerging class in what would become Sierra Leone. The Creoles, descendants of settlers and liberated Africans, were the instruments used by philanthropists and abolitionists in England and elsewhere to establish Freeport as a viable colony. They immediately became an elite and privileged group. Even though many liberated Africans did not succeed, most of these families went on to become community leaders. Europeans remained at the top of the social pyramid, but over time the Creoles developed a prestige rarely seen among tribal Africans. Creole culture was assigned positive social value, while tribal cultures were seen more negatively.

As my father documented, many tribal Africans found it desirable to assimilate and "pass" for Creoles. Fosterage also became common in Freetown. Tribal children were handed off to Creoles, if the families proved willing, so that they might receive a more Western upbringing. My father noted, however, that these children rarely achieved the status or privilege enjoyed by bona fide Creoles.

Within this context, it is fair to say that my family had a slightly different and very Western approach. Growing up, we shared an acknowledged superiority complex. My father had attended Cambridge, where many of the Africans expected to eventually return to run their respective countries and become the established intelligentsia.

At the end of each school year, however, many of these privileged Africans remained in England. They congregated on Brown Street, near Oxford Street, in central London. Like any ethnic neighbourhood, this one had a history of African residents. Common birds tend to flock together. People would sit in cafés and talk politics, discussing what to do in Africa when their countries became free from British or European influence.

I often heard stories of the time my father spent with Robert Mugabe, the long-time leader of Zimbabwe, when they became flatmates in London one summer. I never got to meet Mugabe, but my father described him as very passionate and pan-African. Even back then, Mugabe knew exactly what he wanted for Zimbabwe. Samora Machel, the former president of Mozambique, was also part of that group. Machel was a leading member of the Mozambique Liberation Front, or FRELIMO, the organization that ousted the Portuguese and took over the country.

In one sense, I think my father was divided in his apparent dislike for politicians. He understood the important changes that were occurring in Africa, and I dare say he was equally passionate about the continent's future. At the same time, he had a very European and cosmopolitan view of the world.

My mother's Danish background was equally represented in our home, which was located on the university campus. Our house seemed large, though we often have that impression when we are children. I had my own room, and various people milled in and out, helping out with the domestic duties. It was very common in Sierra Leone to have servants. While the house had an African flavour, much of our furniture came from Denmark. It was modern, clean and functional. Danish design is often simple yet sharp. We were always one of the few families in the neighbourhood to have a real Christmas tree over the holidays.

My mother was also in charge of the kitchen. I suspect she was the only person in Freetown serving Danish delicacies. I remember our dining room table covered in smorgasbord or those famous open-faced sandwiches, usually on dark bread, with cold meats and colourful vegetables piled on top. On special occasions, like Christmas, a typical feast would be steaming platters of roasted pork and potatoes with red cabbage. Sunday lunches, however, were reserved for Sierra Leonean foods, mostly stew, rice and fish. We often had Jollof rice in our household, a one-pot meal with meat or fish sauce. Pepper soups and a variety of dishes cooked with palm oil and green leaves were Sunday staples too.

Preserving our African heritage was important, and I am still a very proud Sierra Leonean. It is a wonderful place and often misunderstood. The coast, where I grew up, is mostly made up of Creoles and people of British origin. The hinterland consists predominately of tribal groups who speak a number of different languages. With a population six million strong, Sierra Leone unfortunately remains a poor country, due to its rather brutal history.

SIERRA LEONE'S greatest assets—its mines—have also been its curse. It has some of the most productive mines in the world. The country is particularly known for its diamonds, but it is also among the largest producers of titanium, baux-ite, gold and rutile. When you fly there, it is common for the plane to be filled with muscular men wearing heavy boots and speaking with English or South African accents. You know they will not be spending too much time on the beach. Sierra Leone is not a tourist destination. These men are going to the mines.

Sierra Leone suffered during Liberia's civil war, which ran from 1989 to 2003. Most people have heard the term "blood diamonds," which essentially refers to diamonds mined in war zones and sold to finance wars. Charles G. Taylor, the president of Liberia, was often accused of sup-porting Sierra Leone's own civil war, which lasted from 1991 to 2002, through the trade of weapons for diamonds across the northern border. The conflict left tens of thousands dead in Sierra Leone and decimated the country's infra-structure. Al-Qaeda was also known for plucking gold and diamonds from these borders, allowing the organization to transfer cash into commodities at a time when its assets were frozen around the world.

Political strife has been an ongoing challenge in Sierra Leone, with mercenaries attempting to take over the coun-try at different stages in our history. So the country has cer-tainly gone through some bad times, but the people elected a good president in 2007: Ernest Bai Koroma. Throughout my career, I have tried to support him and my country from different places in the world. I still believe Sierra Leone has a bright future.

When I was growing up, people loved to laugh. Sierra Leoneans are a happy and generous people, despite their history. Although my memories are scarce, I know that my childhood was happy.

We often ate lunch or dinner on the beach as a family. My father loved to visit our holiday home right on the coast, even though he did not swim. In fact, hardly anyone swam in Sierra Leone. Even the fishermen did not swim. This aversion to swimming is fairly common throughout Africa and indeed the Caribbean. Have you seen many black Olympic swim teams? On the whole, people do not seem too interested. In Sierra Leone, the folklore surrounding "Mami Wata" scared adults and children to death. Mami Wata probably takes on different meanings depending on where you go. When I was growing up, she was known as the devil in the water. If you wandered too far in, she would haul you into her spirit world until you drowned. There were riptides on the coast, and I think this legend was created to keep children safe after a few people died. However, my mother never placed much stock in Mami Wata. As far as she was concerned, my sister and I should be dropped into the water head first once we were strong enough to paddle. My father would stand near the shore, water lapping peacefully around his waist as he watched us splashing and screaming in the crashing waves.

AS A HALF-BLACK and half-white descendant of ex-slaves from the U.S. and Canada, with an African father and a European mother, I have often felt between worlds. My rather rich heritage and personal history have also served me well, however, since people have never quite known where to place me.

My Danish heritage in particular seemed to surprise people. During the 1990s, when I was living with my family in Detroit, I got a strange call from Immigration Services. Suzanna, my teenage niece from Denmark, had just arrived at the airport. She was planning to stay with us in the U.S. as an au pair, so she could learn English. She encountered some problems upon arrival, however, since she lacked a work permit and didn't have the language skills to sufficiently explain herself. I was at the airport waiting for her, when my cell phone rang. Immigration Services was requesting my presence in one of their holding rooms.

An official there gave me a cross-eyed look. He asked pointedly if she, Suzanna, was really my niece. It dawned on me during the car ride home why they had been so suspicious. Here I was, picking up this blonde, blue-eyed eighteen-year-old woman who claimed to be my niece. Many families are multicultural, of course. Nevertheless, those immigration officers made me feel more like a sugar daddy.

My mother ensured that my sister and I learned to speak Danish. Although I have not had the opportunity to use it very much, I did take pleasure in giving at least one lecture in my mother's tongue. Many years ago, I was at a medical society meeting in Denmark to deliver a speech on prostate cancer. As I stepped up to the podium, the crowd, in a collective motion, reached for their headphones, which would provide simultaneous interpretation. I had not planned to speak in Danish, but gazing out at the crowd, I could not help but challenge their expectations. As I launched into my lecture, I saw people doing double takes. A few of them took off their headphones and studied the controls. It was not long before I saw smiles spreading across their faces. They'd realized they could understand me. One physician approached me after the lecture to note what an odd experience it had been. Not only was I speaking in Danish, a language not many foreigners can speak, but I also had a rather unusual country accent, as per my mother's hometown. Still, he told me that it was easier to listen when he closed his eyes. I suppose that I did not look the part.

Race was never an issue for me as a young child. In Sierra Leone, people were racist, but it was mostly among blacks—liberated Africans and those who became Creoles felt they were of better stock than tribal peoples, and there were also numerous classifications within the various tribes, related mostly to where you came from and who your people were. But there was little hatred towards whites, people of mixed race or those perceived to be foreigners. I never felt different or ostracized until my family moved to Kenya.

I WAS EIGHT years old when we arrived in Nairobi. I had spent my childhood up until this point in relative calm. In some respects, the university campus in Freetown was much like a North American suburb. It was quiet and spread out, with lots of children to play with. When father took the job as principal of University College in Nairobi, my life changed completely. In Kenya, race was everything.

The country had just gone through the Mau Mau Rebellion, and anti-British sentiment was at an all-time high. The Mau Mau killed the first Europeans in October 1952. Not long after that, the British declared a state of emergency, carrying out mass arrests and gruesome interrogations. Ground assaults, aerial bombings, detention centres and a powerful propaganda machine proved overwhelming for the Mau Mau, particularly after the capture of rebel leader Dedan Kimathi in October 1956. Although the British managed to smash the uprising, bitterness and segregation lingered. I learned very quickly that Kenyans did not laugh or smile as much as Sierra Leoneans did. They took a hard line—build Kenya, for Kenya.

In Sierra Leone, if you happened to have a job, you worked. You could build the country, but only if you wanted to. There was not the same sense of urgency as in Kenya. It was a much more laid-back attitude.

During the 1960s, everything was acutely and palpably "new Kenya." The school I went to had, the year before, been only for white children. The British flag had been taken down. Now, not only was there integration, but many white parents were also losing their jobs through what was termed "Kenyanization."

Jomo Kenyatta, who became the country's first prime minister in 1963, had spent nearly a decade in solitary confinement in the north following the rebellion. The comparison with Nelson Mandela in South Africa stopped there. Kenyatta had more than a few gripes against the British establishment, and as a result the country was not the most hospitable environment for foreigners. An underlying seething anger had built up towards well-established whites in Kenya.

Sierra Leone was known as the "white man's grave" when it was first colonized by the British. It was jokingly said that if you were assigned to be governor there, you must have done something horribly wrong. Odds were that, within a few months, malaria or some other disease would knock you off. Kenya, by contrast, was filled with fertile land, much of which had been handed out to the colonists. People had come with the intention of staying. So tension and resentment existed on both sides.

For the first time in my life, I felt the sting of racism. Kenya's rough and racially charged history was reflected in its children. The hard feelings were palpable in the schoolyard and the halls. I was clearly different. Everyone quickly learned that my mother was European and my father was African. Being half black and half white, I endured racial slurs and bigotry from both camps. White children uttered the N-word. At the same time, many blacks did not see me as one of them. They wanted the whites out of their country.

The ridicule was not always directed at me, but I never joined in with either the whites or the blacks. How could I? Choosing a side would have placed me at odds with my family and everything I had known. It took time, but my experience in Kenya became a training ground for adult life. It toughened me up, and it also taught me how to network and negotiate between opposing groups. I learned quickly to be a diplomat and slide between different factions. I knew that I would never be fully accepted by either side. But I blended in enough that I could gradually win people over to my way of thinking. I ended up with many friends.

And as a boy, I was always conducting business. When I was twelve, we went to Denmark on a holiday to visit my mother's side of the family. At the time, I was attending an all-boys boarding school in Nairobi, where I was president of the photographic society.

Denmark was a very liberal country, and while I was there an idea struck me. I decided to go into the pornography business. I did not choose this avenue to be sordid or crude. It was simply a matter of supply and demand. Those materials were scarce in Nairobi, and of course, pornography would go over well in an all-boys school.

I took all my pocket money and purchased as many hard-core pornographic negatives as I could. That would give me the ability to print pictures and target a mass market. Upon returning to Nairobi, I locked myself in the school's dark room and set about my task. I made little booklets that could be sold or traded to classmates. The reaction was overwhelming. As a purveyor of such goods, I quickly endeared myself to every boy in that school, regardless of colour. When it came to pornography, skin was skin. I soon became one of the most popular boys there. I never got caught for my underworld dealings. In fact, some of the teachers at the school wanted these booklets as well. It made me realize, among other things, that business deals can be a powerful tool.

Becoming a pornography dealer also solved my bullying problem. To this day, I remember the bully's name—Gitaga.

He was in my class, and for whatever reason, Gitaga did not care for me much. For months I had tried to ignore him. He was much bigger than me, and I knew that I had no chance in a physical encounter. But when he ambushed me in the bathroom one morning and stuck my head in the toilet, I decided that I had had enough.

The next day, in geography class, it was my turn to collect the homework assignments. As I slipped between the rows, I very carefully collected Gitaga's book and inserted three photos that involved women and farm animals. I handed the books to the teacher, and three days later, I saw my old friend Gitaga being led out of school. He had been expelled. He looked up at me before he went, and I just smiled and waved. I learned how to handle myself in those early days, and I always meant business.

3.

FROM CAMBRIDGE TO CANADA

THE FALL OF 1975 was my *Titanic* moment.

I remember the day well. After boarding an old cargo ship, I sprinted to the top deck. My classic trunks were feathers in my hands. Huffing and puffing, three levels later, I dropped them at the railing and peered out over the harbour as the ship's crew hoisted the ramp and fired up the propellers.

It was early morning. The sun was rising over the cranes and fishing boats, all the colours and sounds of Freetown Harbour. The air was already hot and sticky. My mother and father had driven me to the harbour, so there I was leaning over the railings, almost falling over, trying to spot them in the crowd. It might seem like something out of an old film, but the people on that old boat did not know when they would see their loved ones next. We savoured those last moments of contact.

I was eighteen years old, on my way to Cambridge University, and I knew it would be close to a year, perhaps

Christmas, before I would return to Freetown. After a few desperate scans, I saw my parents, along with my sister and a handful of relatives, gazing up at me. I started waving frantically, jumping up and down and blowing kisses. The thick ropes that tied us to the dock were tossed up like confetti, and just like that, the ship began lumbering from the harbour.

I wasn't sure if I would return to Sierra Leone after my education, or travel somewhere else and help to support my homeland from afar. I was a proud African and believed in my country. My father's profession as a historian deepened my appreciation of my heritage.

He had also set the bar rather high, since Cambridge was my father's alma mater. He had been part of that African elite. I already knew that I was to be a doctor, so it was time for me to deliver.

I had always been a very good student. I did not play sports and attend cricket matches. Education was everything when I was growing up. I did, however, have my rebellious side. In addition to my pornography enterprise in Kenya, I had sometimes had trouble relating to my teachers. Rules and discipline are often questioned by sharp minds, and while I had some memorable teachers, I thought the majority were narrow-minded idiots.

But now I was free. I was ready to take on the world. The wind was in my hair and I could taste sea salt on my lips. My entire life was ahead of me. The voyage to Liverpool from Freetown took nine long days. This ship was not huge by today's standards. I shared a cabin with another young man, and we spent a great deal of time reading or playing shuffleboard on the deck.

ONCE WE ARRIVED in harbour, I took the train from Liverpool to Cambridge. The train station at Cambridge was popping with fresh-faced students, a portrait of energy, elation and confusion, asking directions, checking instructions scrawled on paper and running this way and that with clunky trunks in tow. It became clear in those first moments that my next great challenge lay before me. I was used to being at the top of my class. However, these students were also the cream of the crop, wherever they came from. I would not say that I was intimidated, but I was certainly aware that I was no longer a big deal. We were all big fish dropped into an expansive ocean. It was sink or swim, and I had a lot of growing up to do.

We piled into cabs at the station and made our way to the colleges. I was at Selwyn College and had the same room my father had stayed in during his time at Cambridge—B28. (My father had a hand in that.) Selwyn College was all-boys and very civilized. We had someone come in and make our bed in the mornings. At 4 PM, another person gave us afternoon tea. But we also knew how to have fun. The rules stipulated that you could not have visitors in the evening, especially of the female persuasion. Curfew was midnight, but that simply meant you could not use the gate. I became quite adept at scaling walls. At least things had improved since my father's time. Back then, you could not have a woman in your room unless you hauled your bed into the hallway. The dormitory masters felt that a bed was an essential ingredient for companionship. Not so. Akin to hanging a tie on the doorknob, everyone knew what a bed in the hallway signified.

On my first day at Cambridge, the sun was beginning to set by the time I unpacked and met some of my neighbours in the dormitory. I inhaled sharply when I saw them freshening up for dinner. I knew from my father's days that all students at Cambridge dressed up for meals, but I hadn't realized that this meant every man wore a tie snugged neatly on his neck. I did not own a tie at the time. We never wore ties in Sierra Leone. It was too hot there, and ties were not considered part of the national dress.

My first order of business, therefore, was to rush out to the store before dinner to buy some ties. Like many students, I did not have a great deal of money, but I found a second-hand store near campus where I bought a box of fifty ties for £1. I figured that would set me up for years. It was not until I got back to my room that I discovered that they were all tie-your-own bow ties.

It took me a while to fashion a reasonably symmetrical bow tie, so I was late to dinner that night. I certainly made an impression, though. I was the only boy wearing a bow tie, and I have worn one ever since. Not only did the look work for me, it seemed to please others. What did I get after that for every birthday and Christmas? A little box with a bow on top. And what was inside? A brand new bow tie. I never bought myself a bow tie again after Cambridge, but I must have accumulated about a thousand of them. The bow tie became my trademark, so much so that if I wore a regular tie, people looked at me funny. The look became synonymous with Arthur Porter.

POLITICS QUICKLY became a big part of my campus life. When I was not studying, I devoted myself to the Cambridge African Union. Not many Africans were at Cambridge, perhaps only a few hundred out of a total student population of fifteen thousand. But the community was smart and driven, and generally came from big families. During my father's time, African students were preparing to become presidents, prime ministers and senior civil servants in their home countries. Although the situation had changed, these boys were certain to return as leaders in their fields. Many in the union were studying the arts and had a mind for politics. Their countries had recently gone through independence, and they had a real sense of change and possibility.

My position as a science student set me apart. And I knew from the very beginning that I wanted to rise up the union ranks. I spent my first year at Cambridge getting to know the right people and making sure they knew me. By my second year, I already had my eye on the union leadership. Campaigning was a political process in its own right. I networked and got key individuals on my side. I distributed pamphlets with a photo of myself and a small blurb, particularly to the Africans who did not know me well. I even held sherry parties and invited influential members of the union. Ballots were handed out to every member at Cambridge, and sure enough, I was elected president. It was a very nice honour, and it looked good on my curriculum vitae. The union became my social circle, and we often met in pubs, restaurants or other places on campus to discuss politics.

The Cambridge African Union was my first experience of taking on a serious position of leadership. I became popular very quickly and won over my brethren. And even then, I was not afraid to make unpopular decisions. It was not long into my term as president that I found myself at the centre of a controversy.

We were constantly tackling the issue of race relations, and many Africans at Cambridge did not want white South Africans or white Rhodesians in the union. I felt skin colour should not matter; what mattered was what was in the heart. It was like those early days in Kenya all over again. I was once again standing on the fence, half white and half black, trying to guide things to a consensus. Some members tried to oust me as president. Like any good university, Cambridge had a robust student newspaper, and the mini-controversy was soon splashed across its pages. It even made it into the *Cambridge Evening News*. I won that battle. I was able to win over enough black African support to my side. White Africans, for the most part, were no longer seen as particularly influential. Their connections were dying as more countries nationalized and achieved independence.

My argument, however, had been one of philosophy and fairness. If Africa was to move forward, it needed to accept all people who wanted to be a part of it. By excluding white members, I felt, we would only be contributing to the hatred and racism that had stained our history.

Plenty of members believed I was being Pollyanna-ish. What did I know about racism and hatred? In fairness, I probably did not fully understand. While the racial divide had been there while I was growing up, particularly in Kenya, I had never fallen victim to violence or aggressive discrimination. Nevertheless, I held on to my belief that, while we were outside of Africa, we should be thinking about building bridges rather than bringing the fight to distant shores. I wanted our members to be a beacon of what things should be like, as opposed to how things were— or had been.

DURING MY second year at Cambridge, I also met the woman who would become my wife. Pamela Mattock was British, hailing from northern England and studying to be a radiation technologist. The similarities with my mother and father's situation were uncanny—they too had met at Cambridge, where my mother was studying to enter healthcare.

The circumstances under which we met, however, were different. I was usually busy with my studies, but my friends and I had developed a very clear and direct strategy for meeting new women at lunchtime. We would wait for two or more women to sit down on their own, and then we would swoop in. We chivalrously inquired if anybody was dining with them before dropping our trays, knowing full well those seats were not taken. One day, Pamela was one of those young ladies.

She was sitting with two friends, eating a muffin, and I found her attractive and interesting enough to ask her on a date. I would be romanticizing if I said it was love at first sight. We did not see each other every day after that, pining and doting, sending each other love letters, flowers and chocolates. Deep down, though, I think that I always knew she was the right person. It was her patience and consistency that made her stand out.

Pamela understood immediately that I was ambitious and driven. During my nine years at Cambridge, from 1975 to 1984, I earned a bachelor of arts in anatomy, a master's in natural sciences and a medical degree. It was no easy task. I studied mornings, evenings, nights and weekends. I learned to study in my sleep. So for our relationship to work, it would have to be a slow burn. Most women I had met asked me to make a choice right then and there. Pamela was patient.

During the summers, when school was out, I worked in London as a bricklayer and drove a little truck on construction sites. I was paid under the table and received a fair amount of money for my labours. It was hard work, though, running from 6 AM to 8 PM, and I was exposed to the elements. I could always tell the difference between summer and winter by the temperature of the rain. It was no worse, however, than marching to school in the rain back in Sierra Leone. I enjoyed my summers in London. Many other foreign students were in the capital during these months. We were paid at the end of each week, so I had money in my pocket, and we spent our evenings in the pub.

I was so busy that Pamela and I lost touch completely for a couple of years. However, I never forgot about her. We met again at a dinner party about two months before my finals, and picked up right where we'd left off. I wrote my exams, qualified and became a medical intern at the university. Now I felt it was time to settle down, and we started dating more seriously after that. It was not long before we were living together, and about a year later I asked Pamela to marry me. We had a relatively small service in her hometown in Yorkshire. My immediate family from Sierra Leone made the trip. I believe it must have been the first, and perhaps the only, multicultural wedding in that little Methodist church in Bradley. Many of the villagers who were not formally invited guests still came out to see the wedding and all the "colourful" folk from Africa. In the three decades that followed, Pamela would stay by my side no matter where we roamed.

It is a cliché to say that behind every great man is an even greater woman. Sometimes, though, clichés exist for a reason. Pamela could not have pursued a full-time career amid my ambitions. I would never have accomplished what I did without her commitment and patience. She ran our home, took care of our four daughters and created an environment where I was free to strive, pursue and succeed. At times, the one-dimensionality of our respective roles became abundantly clear. When parent-teacher interviews came around, I always made a point of attending, or at least tried to do so, given the importance I placed on education. One year, I told my wife I would meet her at the school once I had finished work. It occurred to me only later, as I prepared to leave, that I did not have the foggiest idea where I was going. I knew the name of the school, but I had never dropped my daughters off or picked them up. I had never attended one of their sporting events or extracurricular activities. I loved my daughters dearly. Nevertheless, dedication to one's career comes at a price. I did find the school that night, after consulting a map and fielding a few panicked phone calls to Pamela. The point is, her supporting role kept us going. In truth, I do not think *support* is the best term. It was an equivalent role, because without it, I would not have been able to function properly.

My Best Man, Kevin Gangar, was a close colleague at Cambridge and hailed from Trinidad and Tobago. He married an English girl as well. Kevin was very interested in travelling, particularly back to his home in the Caribbean, and I believe they tried living there for a while. However, it was always difficult to go "back home" after you married someone locally. It was easier to become part of the English reality, with the comforts of two cars, a great school system and a predictable standard of living.

Pamela had not travelled much before she met me. Some couples believe they can handle overseas living but the reality proves different. Expectations change. Fortunately, Pamela took our international lifestyle in stride. The leap from England did not take long. Shortly after I finished my residency in Cambridge, I was looking to travel somewhere new for my specialist training. I applied to a number of places in the U.K. and Canada. Before I heard from anyone else, I got an acceptance letter from the Cross Cancer Institute at the University of Alberta in Edmonton. I received other offers, but people in Alberta were doing research in areas that I was interested in.

I could not have been more eager to begin, though we got off to a bit of a rough start.

WE STEPPED OFF the plane in Edmonton into the most horrible weather you can imagine. I had spent much of my childhood in the subtropical climate of Sierra Leone and Kenya. Granted, England's weather can be cool, rainy and rather miserable; a Canadian winter, however, can be downright nasty. It was only September, and yet the snow was above my knees. I saw cars with power cords plugged into block heaters to prevent engines from freezing. Car tires were distorted into squares. Pamela and I had one child in tow—our oldest daughter, Gemma—and we slogged our way to our small two-bedroom apartment. We had about $10,000 to our names. For the next four years, I would be making the modest salary of a resident.

Money was tight back then, but we never thought about it in that way. Our needs were simple. We did not have much of a social life. In those early years, I spent long days and nights at the hospital. When I was not there, my head was stuck in medical textbooks. I got used to the harsh weather partly because I was so rarely outside. One thing

I did like about Edmonton, however, was those sunny days and frontier skies. It was far brighter and more wide open than London. It could be quite lovely as long as you did not open a window or a door.

I was about one year into my training when opportunity dropped out of those skies. Every second day I would spend the entire night at the hospital on call. Some nights I slept, other times I never sat down. It was one of the slow nights, around 2 AM, and I was dozing over a textbook when the phone jolted me to attention. On the other end was an officer from the Royal Canadian Mounted Police with a rather unusual request. Like a shooting star, a Russian communication satellite had plunged into a forest near Grande Prairie. The RCMP needed someone to perform a survey to ensure there were not high levels of radiation in the surrounding area.

I was training to become a full radiation oncologist, so I immediately sprang into action. It sounded awfully exciting, though as it turned out, cleaning up after fallen satellites was not the most glamorous job in the world. I had to drive the six hours up to Grande Prairie right then and there. When I arrived, around daybreak, authorities had the area all wired off. There were no fires or suspicious-looking men walking around in space suits or black suits and sunglasses. I never even saw the satellite. People might be surprised to know that satellites fall to earth all the time. It just does not tend to happen in your backyard.

I performed my survey and found the radioactivity to be slightly above normal, but below the range where it would be dangerous. The survey was really more of a precaution on the part of Canadian authorities. The significance, however, was that the incident placed me on their radar. Anyone could have been on call that night at the hospital and picked up the phone. What the experience did was to allow me to showcase my knowledge and my willingness to work. From that day on, I'm sure the RCMP and other government agencies had my number on speed dial. I never got paid for any of these consultations, but I considered them an investment.

My persistence and enthusiasm paid off when I was asked to make a trip to Russia soon after the fall of the Soviet Union. In the late 1980s and early 1990s, Western powers were worried about the considerable stockpile of nuclear warheads lurking behind the Iron Curtain. And once the curtain was lifted, countries such as Ukraine, Latvia and Kazakhstan were suddenly faced with what to do with their arsenals. It was risky and expensive storing atomic bombs and radioactive material. National pride did not allow these countries to just give their arsenals away, so the creation of medical isotopes seemed like the perfect decommissioning stream.

The concept was quite novel. In the past, most disarmament programs had involved simple decommissioning, not redeploying. My role in Russia was to advise those in charge on the steps needed to convert the material in these bombs into medical tools that, theoretically, could have a big impact on the delivery of care. It was a real demonstration of "atoms for peace."

In layman's terms, I explained to the Russians the process of mixing nuclear isotopes with different salts, which caused the isotopes to degrade in a kind of distillation process. I guided delegates down the periodic table, adding neutrons here and taking away protons there, and described the building blocks for creating radioactive material for cancer patients. It was not the most efficient way of generating medical isotopes, but the process was appealing due to the political climate at the time. Later, I would provide similar consultations to the U.S. Department of Energy. I did not get paid for these labours. I enjoyed the work; I never did anything that was not fun. But more to the point, these consultations gave me some political connections and ultimately led to future appointments.

PEOPLE HAVE OFTEN wondered how I accomplished so much in my career in such a short time. The answer is indispensability. In those early years, whether it was at the hospital or in my work with government agencies, I made myself aggressively available. It was far easier for people to have me around than not. No matter that I was missing a child's birthday or my wedding anniversary, or had a bad cold; I was always ready to work. I arrived early and left late. I did my job so well that I was often doing the work of two, three or four people.

To succeed in this world, you need to have smarts and a little bit of luck. You also need to be indispensable. Your presence needs to become priceless. Being constantly present and visible is where the politics comes into play. When I was not seeing patients, studying or dealing with satellites and warheads, my focus was on getting to know the decision makers around me and making sure they understood how indispensable I was. That was probably why, after finishing my training as a radiation oncologist, I was offered a full-time job at the University of Alberta.

From the outset I tried to develop very good connections in the radiotherapy world. My research helped put me on the map. I was best known for my work concerning prostate cancer, in particular the use of brachytherapy, whereby I inserted radioactive material directly into the organ. It was the first time the technique had been done in this fashion. Rather than spend eight weeks in radiotherapy, patients endured just three days with needles surgically implanted in the prostate. Armed with my growing body of research, I threw myself into the national and international seminar circuit. As it turns out, I was just getting warmed up. Over the course of my medical career, I would receive credit for three hundred scholarly works in peer-reviewed journals. I also sat on the editorial board of thirteen scientific publications.

Throughout my life, I have also tried to steer clear of what I call "useless moments." Whenever I did something, I asked myself about its purpose. Time was the greatest commodity, and I was always looking to grow. I never joined the chess club at Cambridge, for example. While chess is a wonderful game, I did not see its value in terms of building my career. Leading the Cambridge African Union, however, had practical merits and implications for my future. I engaged only in activities that would take me forward, not backwards or sideways. Successful people, in my view, consciously build their futures.

THE NEXT STEP for me came in 1988, even sooner than I had expected. I had only spent one year in Edmonton on staff as a senior specialist, but I made that year count. Now the University of Western Ontario was offering me the position of chief radiation oncologist for the London Regional Cancer Program.

At just twenty-nine years old, I was probably the youngest medical chief Western had ever hired, and probably the youngest department chief at any hospital in Canada. To this day, I do not know of anyone else who has achieved this milestone so quickly. It goes without saying that I was the youngest person in my department. I was even younger than some of the residents still training to be full specialists. And yet there I was, bright-eyed and bushy-tailed, coming into a large department with just one year of full-time experience under my belt. I could only imagine how the appointment had gone over with my staff. I would expect there were whispers in corners, a few furrowed eyebrows and a high degree of skepticism. I did not blame people. But I doubt they underestimated me once I arrived. My general philosophies of management are fairly straightforward. To use a military analogy, I fight on the front lines, not at the back.

I was consistently in the fray, getting my hands dirty, ready to do battle. I went out of my way to get as much input from my staff as possible. A good leader must listen and be accessible. However, staff knew that once a decision was final, the book was closed. A very clear strategy was in place if you wanted to be part of the team. I tried to build a mutual respect and camaraderie that was not based on my title or the name on my desk. I respected people if they continued to earn it. For my part, I did not demand respect because of my rank or position; I earned it.

Although I had already achieved a great deal in my field, I must admit I was restless. My family and I lived in a very pleasant house on the outskirts of London. Pamela gave birth to our second daughter, Fiona, and the four of us enjoyed a quiet and traditional Canadian life. Deep down, however, I was not satisfied. I knew the moment I took the job that it was simply a springboard to greater heights. What I really wanted was to lead a much larger department, perhaps in Toronto or somewhere in the U.S. So I continued making speeches, participating in seminars and networking on the international circuit. I shook lots of hands. And within three years of my arrival at Western, I received two job offers in the U.S.

The first was in New Orleans, where I was offered chief of oncology in the Ochsner Health System. I seriously considered it, as the hospital had the reputation of being the Mayo Clinic of the South. I also had a soft spot for the food and culture of New Orleans. Management flew me down there to meet the players. They wined and dined me for a few days. I might have taken the job if it were not for David Duke, the Republican in the Louisiana House of Representatives for that area of the city. We were driving through New Orleans, not far from the hospital, when I saw Duke's face plastered on political posters. It must have been election time.

In addition to being a politician, Duke was known for his strong affiliation with the Ku Klux Klan. In mid-1974 he had founded the Louisiana-based Knights of the Ku Klux Klan and appointed himself "Grand Wizard." The organization slowly evolved during this time, as members shed their hoods and white robes and slipped on suits and ties, endeavouring to become more professional and part of mainstream society. Duke left the Klan in 1980 and formed the National Association for the Advancement of White People. He had won his seat in the Louisiana House Representatives in the 1989 election and would hold the post until 1992. So when I arrived in New Orleans in 1991, a year remained in his term.

Seeing those posters made me a bit uneasy. When I asked my tour guide, who also happened to be a senior manager in the hospital network, about Duke, he said the oddest thing. "Not to worry, Arthur," he smiled, slapping my leg reassuringly. "It doesn't mean much. We were all in the KKK when we were young."

We laughed it off and carried on with the tour. But to me, an African of mixed race, his words meant something. I wasn't yet a Republican myself, but I knew that my relationships with local politicians would be crucial to my success wherever I roamed. So the job prospect in New Orleans did not get off to the best start.

The Detroit Medical Center had come calling at around the same time. My family and I were more than familiar with the Motor City from our cross-border shopping trips. It had one of the largest radiation departments in the U.S., and it was the only place with a superconducting cyclotron. That would mean little to the average person, but for a radiation oncologist, it was the ultimate toy. The National Superconducting Cyclotron Laboratory, located at Michigan State University, was just bringing this new piece of equipment online in the early 1990s. It tickled my fancy, so to speak, because I knew that this research tool could take me to the next level. Nobody else had one, so anything we did on it would be considered novel in some way. Like so many other professions, medicine, and indeed oncology, fall victim to fads and trends.

The job on offer was that of radiation-oncologist-in-chief, as well as chairman and professor of the Detroit Medical Center and Wayne State University. I toured the facilities, met all the players and was very impressed and reassured. Back in London, Pamela and I sat down at the kitchen table to make a final decision on our next step. She asked me questions about what I would be doing and how the family would fit in. We spoke about where we would live and whether any good schools were in the area for the girls. And then she asked me: How much does it pay? I had no idea. While money tended to accompany success, it was never the driving force behind my decisions. I assumed, in my ascension to bigger roles, that higher compensation would follow. Nevertheless, it was an important question that had simply never come up in the job interviews.

I got up from the table and called the president of the hospital and dean at the School of Medicine that very night.

I told him how interested I was in the appointment. My wife and family were excited about the prospect, too. But how much did the job pay?

"I have no idea," Dean Sokol said.

My position at the Detroit Medical Center, you see, was my first experience with commercial medicine. In Canada, where healthcare is bound to the public sector, it was always very clear what I would bring home. My new boss-to-be told me that, as chairman, I would form a company, hire my staff and bill the patients. I was chief in every sense of the word. If no money was left over after salaries, equipment and overhead, then I would not get paid. Of course, establishing the largest oncology department in the state of Michigan would require some start-up cash. The dean suggested that I take out a mortgage on my house.

When I returned to the kitchen table and told Pamela there was no formal salary, and we would need to mortgage the house just to get started, she nearly slid off her chair. It was not the most traditional financial plan. I was only thirty-two years old, with two kids. If I accepted the post, I would become one of the youngest people ever to reach full professor status in Canada or the U.S.

It was no ordinary move. But the risks never stopped me. Although I was wary of what lay before me, I was always ready to take on the world.

The Detroit Medical Center was a wild leviathan compared to where I had come from. More importantly, it would be my first foray into business. I have never been a sports fan, but a certain analogy seemed particularly apt. The London Tigers were a professional AA baseball team that played in Canada from 1989 until 1993. They were the farm team to the Detroit Tigers. In many respects, after rising quickly on the Canadian scene, I too was being called up.

It was time for the big leagues.

4.

"THE MOST POPULAR MAN IN DETROIT"

I HAD THE BEST parking spot at the Detroit Medical Center. Nestled in the corner on the first-floor parking deck, right beside the door leading to the elevator, it was perfect during those freezing winter months or when I was in a rush to get back to the office. Everyone at the hospital knew where I parked my white Jaguar xjs with its distinctive blue soft-top.

And on that spring morning in 1999, that was exactly the problem.

It was the hole in my windscreen that caught my attention. I was late for a meeting downtown, but the situation was strange enough to stop me in my tracks. Something did not feel right. I stood there for a moment, keys in hand, my head bent slightly to the side. I studied the hole a little more closely. From a distance, it looked like a bad chip, as if a rock had flown up from the road and cracked the glass. But as I peered in through the driver's side window, I saw another hole in the centre of the headrest—right where my head would be, between the eyes. I shook my head in disbelief. It was not a chip at all. It was a bullet hole.

I squatted down beside the car and scanned my surroundings. One or two people were farther down the parking deck, heading for their cars. Nothing seemed amiss. Was I going crazy? I did not know what to think. The only thing I knew for certain was that I would not be making that meeting downtown.

I retreated indoors, heading for my office, and called security from there. It was not long before city police and the FBI got involved. After all, I was no ordinary radiation oncologist. Much had changed since my move to Detroit in 1991.

SOON AFTER THAT kitchen table discussion in London, my wife and I had taken the financial plunge. We got a mortgage on our new house in Detroit so that I could take the job. After all, it would be three months or so before the first patients, and their insurance companies, paid their bills. Until then, I had to single-handedly cover all my doctors' salaries and the overheads. I was nervous in the beginning, though I was also confident about my abilities. By the end of my first year, the radiation department at the Detroit Medical Center was rolling. Within a couple of years I had set up other clinics and radiation centres in Michigan and northern Ohio. As it turned out, the business of medicine, and indeed business in general, suited me quite nicely.

As in Canada, I remained on the seminar circuit. I gave talks throughout North America, built contacts and pumped out research papers for noted academic journals. I loved my job. To be honest, I never entirely saw myself as a healthcare administrator. I was a successful physician. I took great pleasure in seeing patients. Unlike shareholders, politicians or a boardroom full of executives, patients have a singular knack for making you feel good. I discovered too that people respected doctors but loathed healthcare administrators. In the latter role, you only received attention when something went wrong. As a doctor, you had twenty minutes to make an impression during the first consultation. It was not so different from a business transaction. In that limited amount of time, I had to convince this person, who might be teetering towards death, that they should turn their body over to me. I had to connect with them. It was a hell of a deal to strike.

BY 1999, EIGHT years into my tenure at the Detroit Medical Center, I had been appointed president of the American Brachytherapy Society and president of the American Cancer Society's Michigan division. I had had the distinction of being named a "Michigander of the Year." I was also the first president of the American College of Radiation Oncology to have been born outside the U.S. My plate was full—heaping, in fact. But as Pamela often said, I was still on the lookout for the next big thing.

One day, David Campbell, the president and CEO of the Detroit Medical Center, came storming down the hall. I was doing rounds with an entourage of oncologists, residents and interns in tow as he stormed past me in a pale grey suit, huffing and puffing. His face was so red I expected blood to spew out his ears. It was not long before whispers reached me.

News was spreading like a superbug. David had just been fired.

Detroit's economy was in the doldrums, and the situation was getting worse. Overseas competition had put the brakes on Motor City's most coveted industry. Put simply, the big three car companies—General Motors, Chrysler and

Ford—had not kept up with the rest of the world. They were still making big, gas-guzzling vehicles marked by comparatively shoddy workmanship. Cars out of Japan and Europe had become cheaper and more appealing. These titanic U.S. firms could not change course fast enough. They were too big and slow to avoid a catastrophic economic collision. The decline of the big three spilled over and touched everyone in the city. I would sometimes drive through downtown and stare at the abandoned and boarded-up buildings; it was like I was visiting an entirely different country. The population of Detroit fell to below one million. Geographically, it continued to resemble a donut. While the suburbs were getting full, fat and prosperous, in the middle was a void, at best a few crumbs. Unlike Chicago and New York City, the Greater Detroit region was made up of independent cities, each with its own fire brigade, police department and tax system.

Bloomfield Hills, a community just over thirty kilometres from downtown Detroit, has consistently ranked in the top five wealthiest U.S. communities with populations of between 2,500 and 10,000. When I lived in Michigan, it was ranked second in the U.S. It had sparkling schools, beautiful churches and a host of celebrity residents. Shortly after I arrived in Detroit, a very senior politician was quoted as saying that he had no problem with the stark differences between this community and Detroit city proper. He would be happier, however, if the people of Bloomfield moved to Detroit as often as those in Detroit moved to Bloomfield. Many of Bloomfield's residents were leading executives in the auto industry or barons of other businesses in Detroit. If you want to live in this wonderful place, the politician said, don't move to Detroit to work and then take your money a couple dozen miles out to build mansions and country clubs.

As a resident of Grosse Pointe Farms, a town akin to Bloomfield Hills and home to some of the most affluent families in Michigan, I thought his point was well made. Bloomfield and Grosse Point Farms were just two of many prosperous communities that were cut off from the downtown core. Amalgamation would have made sense. But who wants to take on an almost bankrupt partner? (And in July 2013, the city of Detroit did indeed file for bankruptcy.) The historical cleavages only made the income divide more profound. There were other divisions as well. Downtown Detroit was mostly black. The suburbs were white. Downtown tended to have a higher concentration of Democrats, as did the state of Michigan at large. The more prominent citizens of these suburbs were Republican.

The Detroit Medical Center was special, since it did not have the same clearly defined borders. This network, the largest employer in Detroit, represented seven hospitals, twenty-one thousand employees and $2 billion in annual revenue. However, it was hemorrhaging from every orifice. A struggling healthcare system was perhaps the biggest symptom of Motor City's economic jam. By 1999, we were losing between $500,000 and $1 million every month. One of the biggest reasons for these gargantuan losses was the $120 million to $150 million in uncompensated care dished out every year to the good people of Michigan. In tough times, medical insurance is often the first thing to go. While hospitals in the suburbs had kept their heads above water, the inner city was suffering terribly.

The Emergency Medical Treatment and Active Labor Act, or EMTALA, specified that hospitals could not turn away a critically ill patient or a patient in labour, medical insurance or not. The deterioration of Detroit, and the consequent rise in poverty and unemployment, only made the situation worse. If an uninsured male stumbled into a hospital with a gunshot wound to the chest or with any other serious ailment, we were obligated to treat him. The hospital picked up the tab.

The link between medical care, Detroit's automotive industry and the broader economy ran even deeper. The automotive companies were considered good employers, in terms of both salary and benefits. But when the economy tanked, it made their business models unfeasible. Toyota, for example, had around $250 built into every car for the provision of healthcare; in other words, that was the cost of providing medical benefits to their employees. Health-care benefits at General Motors, Ford and Chrysler, on the other hand, represented a whopping $2,000 per car. That $2,000 was applied to the final price tag of every vehicle that rolled off the assembly line. General Motors alone paid full medical benefits for nearly 250,000 employees and their dependants.

The Detroit Medical Center was indeed an economic linchpin. It was no wonder the automotive companies were constantly dealing with the healthcare sector, searching for ways to reduce costs. Despite all the tweaking and shifting, however, only so much could be done. The entire system was on its knees.

The board of directors at the Detroit Medical Center had had enough. Change was needed, and David Campbell's head was on the chopping block. In the U.S., healthcare was a cash business. It ran like a corporation. If you did not make your margins, you were out.

That was where I came in. My star was rising at the centre, not just as a radiation oncologist, but also as a businessman.

I had run a large and profitable department for years and expanded my brand beyond the hospital network. So I was not entirely surprised when the board of directors requested my presence on the same day I'd seen David storming past.

More than a dozen suits watched me enter the boardroom in my white doctor's coat with a stethoscope around my neck. The board of directors represented a corporate powerhouse, men who ran big companies and banks in the state. Nonetheless, I felt totally at ease. Although I had expected that my number might be called, I had never believed I would be given the final nod. It was a high-profile position. My experience in business was relatively new, and I had certainly never run an organization posting billions in annual revenue. The appointment was also very political in nature. It would become a popularity contest once it got out in the mainstream. But in that moment, the blood was still on the walls. The board was searching for answers. It was the perfect time to strike.

First, the board offered me an interim position while it conducted a more thorough search for the next president and CEO. I would be a Band-Aid, a quick and temporary fix.

Turning to Eugene Miller, the head of Comerica Bank and chairman of the board, I thanked him, but said "no." If the board wanted to hire me, that was fine, I said, but not as an interim. I knew I would be vulnerable in that position, especially once other candidates began circling.

Miller smiled and asked me to leave the room. The great thing about being a doctor was that I already had a successful career. Anything else was gravy at that point. I went back to work, and within a few hours I was called back to the boardroom. The board appointed me the new president and CEO of the Detroit Medical Center.

Amid a flurry of applause and handshaking, Miller put his arm around me and led me into a corner.

"Arthur, do you know what CEO stands for?" he whispered.

"Of course I do, Gene. I'm the chief executive officer." I smiled. "The man in charge. Captain of the ship, so to speak."

"I'm afraid not." He shook his head.

"Then what?"

"It stands for the three things you now need to think about every day—Clients, Employees and *Own-ers*." He placed extra emphasis on the latter, squeezing my shoulder.

My professional life would never be the same. The Detroit Medical Center was not a state hospital; the owners expected profitability. But beyond that, I was now in charge of the biggest employer in all of Detroit, a city on the ropes. And with that came power. I was no longer just a doctor and businessman. I had been dropped into the political machine with the levers of control in my grasp.

It was not exactly a plum job. I knew that within less than twelve months of my taking over the system, the centre would be bankrupt at the current rate of deterioration. And I knew I could not save it on my own. We brought in the Hunter Group, a corporate advisory firm out of Florida known for kicking an organization in the balls, so to speak, and getting its fiscal house in order. They explained the situation to me in a way I could immediately understand. Think of the Detroit Medical Center as a patient, they said, a patient who has been brought in with serious trauma, bleeding from every extremity. How do you deal with that?

Well, the first step, of course, was to stop the bleeding— or, in this case, the spending. Spending could be broken down into two main areas: staff and supplies; what I liked to call the dreaded ss. You could not really cut down on supplies, so the only option to bring about real financial change was to reduce staff.

Within six months, I had slashed the staff of the Detroit Medical Center by seven thousand people, from twenty-one thousand to fourteen thousand. I was the most popular man in Detroit. It helped to balance the books, but it came at a personal cost.

THE REALITY OF my new position was hammered home that spring morning as I sat in my office, surrounded by Detroit police and the FBI. No doubt about it, my Jaguar had been shot up. It was a warning. You could not lay off seven thousand people in Motor City, in an already depressed economy, without mucking up the gears. And I was not getting too much sympathy from the authorities either.

"Nobody is really happy with what you're doing," one of the officers said.

"That much is clear," I responded dryly.

"Don't worry, though," another officer chimed in. "This kind of thing happens. In the U.S., one or two CEOs get killed each year."

"That's comforting," I said, rolling my eyes. I leaned back in my chair and looked out the window. "So what should I do?"

"Well, you can get trained," the second officer said. "You can buy a gun."

"I own guns. I already know how to use them. What else?"

An FBI agent stepped forward. "I recommend getting a driver."

He was using the term "driver" rather loosely. Later that day, I met with one of our senior security personnel, Earl "the Pearl" Weems, in my corner office.

I knew immediately that he was the right man for the job. The Pearl was a retired cop, well over six feet tall, with dark wraparound sunglasses. He wore a blue suit, a matching tie and a Beretta 9mm pistol strapped to his waist.

I parked the Jaguar at home in my garage, permanently, and swapped it for a black Cadillac. From then on, whenever I needed to go somewhere, I called the Pearl for a pickup. We did not have a set routine, partly because of my schedule, but also to keep any would-be assassins guessing. Sometimes he would meet me at the back or side door. Other times he pulled right up to the front. Pamela and I bought a house outside the city, and I kept an apartment downtown for those nights I worked late and could not get home. It was a strange feeling having a bodyguard at first, though I quickly realized that it was an excellent way to catch up on paperwork. Earl "the Pearl" Weems was a quiet giant and not much of a conversationalist, which suited me just fine. I spread out on those black leather seats and got a great deal done driving back and forth from the office or between meetings.

I have never believed that life is a popularity contest. I have often agreed to take on hard things and make difficult decisions. Do I enjoy being liked? Sure, everyone does. But do I get upset when someone does not like me? No, not particularly.

It bothered me on occasion when I was splashed across Detroit's newspapers, day in and day out, and portrayed as public enemy number one. It made my job more difficult when what I was trying to do was take a stand and fight for something. If I had wanted to, I could have retired as the medical centre's president and CEO. I could have continued on as many people do, going to work in the morning, leaving in the afternoon, performing adequately and without controversy. That was the way most healthcare systems worked. I would have returned at some point to my position as chief of radiation oncology and held down a lucrative practice.

It is when you try and change something that people start rejecting you. I believe, however, that if you have everyone onside, you are probably not doing a very good job. If you can split that public opinion, then perhaps you are beginning to accomplish something worthwhile.

If people had not known me in Detroit before, they knew me now. However, I was something of an enigma. Was I American, Canadian or African? The blacks in Detroit thought I was one of them. Whites thought I spoke well, and given my background and complexion, they thought I must be of their ilk. A few years after I arrived in Michigan, I had been invited to join the Country Club of Detroit—the most exclusive golf club in the city. I did not play much, really. It was more of a place to hold meetings and network. To me, restaurants and clubs were like hotels and political parties: when I found a place I liked, I stuck with it until I was so well known that it paid off. After I'd joined the country club, one of the oldest members came up to me at the bar and told me I was the first. The first what? I asked him. The first radiation oncologist? The first Canadian?

I knew exactly what he meant, though; I suspect that I was the first black man to join the country club. But I did not stop there. I was also a member of the Detroit Club and the Detroit Athletic Club. Both became essential stomping grounds for conducting business—places to be seen. Every insurance or automotive executive worth knowing belonged to these clubs. The big deals happened at the bar, over lunch or perhaps during chance conversations in the hallways.

Even after the widespread layoffs, I had my allies in Michigan. John Engler, the state's Republican governor, was a friend and confidante during my first two years as the medical centre's president and CEO. I tried to impress on people the dire finances at the centre. It was not seven thousand people leaving. It was fourteen thousand employees staying on. And we turned around a loss of $8 million in the first year to nearly break even in the second.

My work was not done, however. The Hunter Group's analogy of the hemorrhaging patient had a second part. We had stopped the bleeding by squeezing the staff. The second phase was making the Detroit Medical Center as efficient as possible. It was time to effect the cure.

I had been hotly criticized following the layoffs for trying to run things on a shoestring budget. In a sense, my critics were right. When you have fewer people delivering care, the service will inevitably deteriorate. So I knew what I had to do next—close hospitals. In my view, it was the only way to make the health network financially stable. But before this plan could go forward, I had to break the news to my roughest critic.

KWAME KILPATRICK served as Detroit's mayor from 2002 until 2008. Prior to that he had been a member of the Michigan House of Representatives. In some respects, Kilpatrick was very much a reflection of his parents. His mother, Carolyn Kilpatrick, was a career politician, and his father, Bernard, was a semi-professional basketball player. I believe Bernard Kilpatrick dabbled in politics as well. Like his father, the mayor also had an athletic streak; he had been a linebacker in college.

Kwame Kilpatrick had a rather colourful history, and a number of scandals broke during his time as mayor. Years later, he would be forced to resign his post after being found guilty of perjury and obstruction of justice. Those charges proved to be only the beginning. He would later be convicted of mail fraud, wire fraud and racketeering involving some of the most prominent citizens of Detroit.

Perhaps the most publicized scandal, dubbed the Manoogian Mansion party by the press, involved an alleged soiree at the mayor's home in 2002. Former members of his personal Executive Protection Unit claimed they had arrived at the residence with the mayor's wife, at which point various abuses towards strippers in attendance allegedly took place.

The party incident opened up a can of worms concerning the Executive Protection Unit, but a full-scale investigation was cut short. Less than a year later, one of those same strippers was shot multiple times while in a car with her boyfriend, and a major scandal broke loose over the possible involvement of the Detroit Police Department. One high-ranking officer signed an affidavit implicating the police department in the stripper's murder. Another signed an affidavit confirming links between the stripper, the mayor of Detroit and the mayor's wife.

My dealings with Kilpatrick were limited, though the hospital did receive the occasional phone call from the Executive Protection Unit and the chief of police. These calls, usually made to me or to one of my top executives, would often come in the middle of the night, telling me that so-and-so was coming into the hospital and asking me to make sure the blood alcohol reading was normal—not the easiest thing to arrange. Sometimes there were fights or other incidents for which the authorities did not want an official medical report. They specified that the patient should be given a private room or led out the back door so the media did not get a sniff of a story.

I mention this history only to demonstrate that Kilpatrick was not a man to be trifled with. I thought he was a bit of a bully. He did not like me, and I did not like him. I suppose we could not have been any different. Here I was, of Cambridge background, a scientist and a businessman, polished, well travelled and well educated. I was the son of an academic. I prided myself on my decorum and my networking and negotiation skills. Kilpatrick, on the other hand, was rough around the edges. In Detroit he was considered a man of the people. He was brash and unapologetic.

I asked to meet with Kilpatrick at the Detroit Athletic Club, in the boardroom on the second floor. Pitchers of water were sweating in the middle of the table. I had chosen that club for two reasons. First, as noted, business was often conducted in these venues. More importantly, it was a public place. I knew there could be fireworks following the announcement I was about to make. I was a bit nervous. In one corner sat the scowling Kilpatrick, arms crossed, sporting one of his patented muscle shirts, pecs, biceps and triceps bulging, as if he had just come from the gym. He was a large man, well over six feet tall. The bodyguards flanking him, however, were even larger. In my corner was Susan Capatina, my chief of staff, a woman in her early forties. She was a lovely person, but not exactly the most intimidating backup.

So there was Susan in her business suit and me in my bow tie as I told the mayor we would be closing two inner-city hospitals within ninety days.

Kilpatrick sprang across the table, knocking over a sweaty pitcher, and grabbed me by the collar. In the heat of the moment, I actually thought he was going to hit me. His bodyguards must have thought so too, because they quickly pulled him off me. He collapsed back into his chair with wild eyes, uttering every insult under the sun.

"I'm gonna get you, Porter!" he screamed. "You're gonna do what you're gonna do! But I'm gonna do what I gotta do!"

Had all hell not broken loose, I would have explained to Kilpatrick that it was better to have fewer hospitals with a certain quality, than to keep all of the facilities open and have insufficient resources. But once Kilpatrick's security pulled him off me, Susan and I briskly made for the exits. I wanted to find an even more public place in case he took another run at me. I didn't relish the prospect of a broken jaw. Visions of Gitaga, the horrible bully from my boyhood back in Kenya, ran ominously through my head. This time, the situation was infinitely more complex. Slipping pornography into his homework would not eliminate Kilpatrick. And I felt this mayor was capable of much more than sticking my head in a toilet. Firing seven thousand workers was one thing. But closing inner-city hospitals in rough-and-tumble Detroit, a city already on the brink of economic collapse, was serious business.

By now, I also had more than the mayor of Detroit to worry about. In 2003, following my first two years as president and CEO, Jennifer Granholm, a Democrat, had been elected as Michigan's new governor.

GRANHOLM HAD BEEN born in Vancouver, British Columbia, but her family moved to California when she was four years old. Before her election as governor, she had served as the attorney general of Michigan, and in later years she would be an economic advisor and part of the transitional team when President Barack Obama came into office. Granholm was very capable. However, not surprisingly, we were not the best of friends.

In a way, I was glad that John Engler was no longer governor. I'd always known what it would take to balance the books at the Detroit Medical Center, and it would have been difficult to enact those reforms under a Republican. Granholm and I were immediately at odds, so that made my demands a bit easier. I told her flat out that either the government taxed the rich hospitals in the suburbs, or the medical centre needed a government funding mechanism to cover the patients we treated who were unable to pay. My announcement did not spark a near-fistfight this time around. What ensued could better be described as a frosty war of wits and words.

I could tell from her response that Granholm thought I was bluffing at first. According to my sources, the same level of skepticism ran deep throughout the city. But at that point, I had already crossed the Rubicon. I needed to show people I meant business, so I took every course of action to back up my plans. I called a press conference and invited every media outlet in Detroit. There I announced that since nobody wanted to pay the medical centre for the uncompensated healthcare at our inner-city hospitals, we were being forced to close both Detroit Receiving Hospital and Hutzel Women's Hospital. I also recommended, with tongue in cheek, that the city cancel the North American

International Auto Show, held in Detroit annually, since there would no longer be a tier-1 trauma centre available. That got people's attention, since the show generated millions in revenue for the city. The media went berserk.

It only added to the general uproar as news of my plan spread. Citizens feared that tens of thousands of people would be left dying in the streets. But I stuck to my guns. I told the critics that it was not my problem. The bigger picture was an issue for the state's Ministry of Health. My problem was making sure that quality was maintained in all the hospitals I ran. I would later be branded as callous and out of touch. But the Detroit Medical Center was a business, plain and simple, and my job, the reason I was hired, was to serve up a dose of reality. And that new reality was bitter going down.

It was high-stakes business with a political twist, which suited me just fine. By this time, shortly after the election of George W. Bush, I was becoming an established player in the Republican arena. I could see my place in the party growing from the municipal and state level to some of the highest offices in the land—but more on that later.

Back in Michigan, what followed was a frenzied back-and-forth in the press. Jennifer Granholm, surrounded by her brain trust in Lansing, had to demonstrate that my demands were unreasonable. There was little debate about the problem of uncompensated care, so the governor sought other reasons for why we needed the money.

She ordered an audit of the Detroit Medical Center. Gross mismanagement was why we needed a bailout, she said. Arthur Porter was trained as a radiation oncologist—what does he know about budgets? *Granholm Slams DMC over Deficit.* The *Montreal Gazette* would later publish stories also accusing the Detroit Medical Center of running high deficits during my tenure, without considering where we came from, the difficulties we found ourselves in and the millions we lost each year from uncompensated healthcare.

That knocked the ball into my court. I slammed the governor, pointing out that the medical centre's deficit was far less than the deficit the state of Michigan had run since she took over. *Porter Hits Back at Governor.*

During television interviews, I would end by writing the figure $150 million on a piece of paper and showing it to the cameras. "Send money," I would say.

The situation went on like this for several weeks. The governor and I were slinging mud, and things were getting messy. Nevertheless, skepticism remained. People wondered whether I would actually do what I threatened or if life would simply return to normal once the governor and I had had enough of the media circus. They were wrong to doubt me. I took this circus on the road. One fine morning in Detroit, around three thousand workers at two inner-city hospitals were handed pink slips and given thirty days' notice.

Suffice it to say the rhetoric reached a new level. I had never been more thankful for Earl "the Pearl" Weems and his black Cadillac. I thought about asking him to carry a machine gun, but instead, I just made myself scarce. Information flowed through bush telegraphs. Rumours flew back and forth.

I know my enemies had intelligence within my inner circle—basically, anyone who was a Democrat—so I rarely went to the office. I scheduled meetings in different places, and the meetings were always structured. I made sure I knew in advance exactly who would be there. I wanted the participants to be balanced so I would not be outnumbered.

Meanwhile, I kept explaining that we did not want to close the hospitals. I showed them the numbers, pushed the economic realities and demonstrated why the current system was unsustainable.

Some people listened, but there was a great deal of hostility, especially as we counted down those thirty days towards the layoffs. There was no turning back. The centre even held job fairs for the three thousand workers about to lose their jobs. As time marched on, my board started to get nervous. Was I sure I wanted to take on the city, the county and the state all at once? I did not have many friends. It soon became clear that, if I could pull this off, it would be my final act as president and CEO of the Detroit Medical Center.

Privately, even I had my doubts about whether the governor would come around. Which of us would blink first? I always prided myself on making tough decisions, holding the line and bending those around me to a certain way of thinking. But a lot was at stake. What if I actually had to close these hospitals? How would the city respond? One hospital was the city's only tier-1 trauma centre, and the other delivered thousands of babies each year, many of them born to mothers who were considered high risk. I wondered at times if I had overplayed my hand.

We were just days from closing the hospitals when I got a call at home. It was Richard Weiner—Dick Weiner, I liked to call him—the governor's chief of staff. Weiner told me to meet him, alone, at a nondescript government building downtown at 8 PM. It would be just the two of us, he said. I thought about taking the Pearl along, just to be safe. In the end, I decided to go it alone. I had a good feeling about this, and it turned out that I was right.

Weiner sat down with me that night and said the governor was planning to propose a $150-million bailout package. It needed approval from the city and the county, although support in principle had already been established. If approved, the bailout would arrive at the eleventh hour. However, a few provisos were attached. The governor was insisting that her people write all the press releases announcing the deal, to handle how the message was delivered. I agreed, on the condition that one of my people was involved for accuracy. We also agreed on a non-defamation clause. I would not say anything bad about them, and they must do the same. Finally, the $150 million would not go just to the Detroit Medical Center. As I recall, the centre received $50 million initially. The governor had to save face, so the package was billed as being for the city. It was not for Arthur Porter.

True to the governor's word, a few days later we held a press conference to announce the Committee for Detroit Healthcare Renewal. We did a big photo shoot, with Granholm, Kilpatrick and me on a stage, all laughing, smiling and shaking hands. My smile was genuine. I had won. However, I knew that it was the end of my Detroit story. I was carrying too much lead, and after that late-night meeting with Weiner, I had gone home to Pamela and told her that I needed to move on. There was bad blood now—things could never be the same. I was tired anyway, and in a sense I had already completed what the board of directors had hired me to do.

The safety net that had been set up would remain in place after my resignation. And when Barack Obama won the next presidential election and introduced healthcare reform, what happened? The government now covered all uninsured patients. Suddenly, there was no uncompensated care in the city of Detroit. By then, the Detroit Medical Center was already running on an efficient shoestring budget. It was ripe for the picking, and it was not long before a private group took it over.

The media would later say I left under "a cloud"—which I suppose I did, considering the political games we played. There would also be claims that Detroit Medical Center suffered huge losses while I was CEO. Those people probably weren't factoring in the millions bled in uncompensated care each year. The fact is, the Detroit Medical Center was in dire straits. And I wrenched it from bankruptcy.

ONCE I'D HANDED in my resignation, I retreated to my home in the Bahamas. My wife and children were pretty well installed there already. For the next six months, my life entered a period of relative calm, far removed from my recent political battles, though the work never stopped. In 2002, I had begun construction of the Cancer Centre in the Bahamian capital of Nassau. I had promised Prime Minister Perry Christie a state-of-the-art medical clinic that would rival counterparts in the U.S., and with the help of a few local physicians, I delivered on that promise. Construction on the clinic was completed in late 2003, shortly before my departure from Detroit. Now that I was based in Nassau, I started seeing patients at the clinic. In addition, I was constantly making deals elsewhere in the world and running my other businesses. Even so, it was not long before I started missing the trenches. To be honest, it was only a few weeks before I was searching for my next battle.

In Detroit, I had reached the peak of my profession, run a billion-dollar enterprise and played some serious politics.

I'd learned a great deal from the experience, not least of which was that I loved the battle. By fighting a messy war and coming out on top, I developed a reputation for dealing with tough, complex and unpleasant situations, or what I liked to call the "big uglies." But my restlessness wasn't only about that. As hinted at earlier, my star had been rising in Republican circles, well beyond the battlefield of Detroit.

5.

"IT IS BETTER KNOWING THE KING"

THE SECRET SERVICE arrived at my office one afternoon in early 2001. Two men marched into the room and sat down stoically across from me, black suitcases on their laps. They were clean-shaven, with military haircuts. They wore crisp white shirts, black ties and black suits. They proceeded to pepper me with questions about nearly everything, from when I stopped wetting the bed to what I had for breakfast that morning. But I was not nervous. In fact, I enjoyed myself. These officers had a job to do, and they were going out of their way to call me "sir." After all, as far as they knew, I could soon be their boss.

I was being considered as the next surgeon general of the U.S. I had achieved a great deal in my career to date, but this appointment would definitely top the list. The U.S. surgeon general shapes healthcare policy on the grandest scale for the most powerful country in the world. He or she is selected by the president and becomes the head of the U.S. Public Health Service Commissioned Corps, taking on the title of vice admiral. For someone in my profession, it was hard to imagine a more prestigious post. It would be the icing on the cake for this boy from Sierra Leone. Indeed, it was the kind of opportunity one only fantasizes about. I had never believed it would come true.

And yet there I was, being respectfully interrogated by the U.S. Secret Service at the Detroit Medical Center. The process was known as a full field investigation, which essentially meant the agency was free to probe me about each and every detail of my life. In addition to the interviews, there was a rather extensive application process. One question, 17B, asked me to list how many intimate affairs I had had since the age of eighteen, including names and dates. That section of the questionnaire had only three lines, but fortunately an additional sheet was provided in case the answers spilled over.

The agents wanted to know if I had any unregistered nannies working for me in the U.S. There had been problems with senior government appointees hiring illegal aliens. The agents also asked if I had any current girlfriends—or boyfriends, for that matter. Were there any extramarital affairs that could get in the way? Sometimes the questions were far less specific. Was there anything they should know about my past or present that could be a cause for embarrassment to the president?

THE FIRST TIME I met George W. Bush, in 1999, he was Governor Bush, and I found him to be fairly unimpressive. I was attending a Republican reception in Washington, D.C., and Bush did not fill the room when he entered. Someone had to poke me on the shoulder and tell me, hey, that's Bush over there in the corner, governor of the state of Texas.

When I took the position as president and CEO of the Detroit Medical Center, I knew that I would be more than a businessman and healthcare administrator. I would routinely be dealing with political figures from the city of Detroit, Wayne County and the state of Michigan. As it turned out, John Engler, Michigan's Republican governor when I first took the post, and I got along quite famously. We had similar ideas and strategies when it came to healthcare, and he supported me when I had to fire seven thousand or so employees during my first few months at the helm.

Getting involved in the political arena was expected of someone in my position. It was also consistent with my natural tendency to network, to bring people together and develop connections. I was never content to sit on the sidelines and let other people make decisions for me. I needed to be part of those decisions. I wanted to shape them. I had joined Canada's Conservative Party when I lived in Alberta, and Republican fiscal policies were in line with my way of thinking. So after arriving in Detroit, I became a member of the Republican Regents, a select group that helped fund the party on the state and the national levels. I had also been elected president of the American College of Radiation Oncology, the American Brachytherapy Society, the American College of Oncology Administrators and the American Cancer Society (Great Lakes). Every so often I travelled to Washington for conventions and to lobby Congress and the Senate on various healthcare bills of the day, serving as an advocate for the body of physicians under my umbrella.

The reception at which I met George W. Bush that day in Washington was a typical Republican Regent event, intended to shore up support and bring us all together. At the time, Bush was considered the clear front-runner for the Republican nomination in preparation for the election the following year. I watched him from afar for a few minutes as I continued speaking with a group of people.

A couple of years before, I had met President Bill Clinton during a private reception at the home of a prominent businessman in Washington. About fifteen of us were there that night. Clinton wanted to talk with us, as physicians and administrators, about his healthcare strategy. I knew the gentleman hosting the party quite well, so there I stood, chatting and sipping wine, waiting for President Clinton to arrive. The Secret Service was already on the scene, along with a number of limousines and an impressive array of hardware, including telephones and briefcases that no doubt had codes and the dreaded red button inside. When Clinton marched into the room, the space lit up. He must have been briefed on everyone at the party, because he moved from person to person easily, and delivered a few personal words with each of us, as if he'd known us for years. The approach was transparent, yet remarkable in its effectiveness. "Bill Clinton knows me. What a wonderful person he is." He made you feel very good about yourself. There was no question, Clinton knew how to work a room. I have never seen anyone do it quite like that. I was a Republican through and through, but Clinton was a master.

Bush did not have the same impact. From a distance, he seemed small, almost diminutive. He smiled a lot, a Texas grin that appeared charming yet anxious. When I finally got to speak with him, however, I found Bush to be equally capable of relaxed conversation. He was not formal, and he could relate easily to people, usually through the use of a parable or a sharp joke to illustrate a larger point. Clinton was slick and structured. I found Bush straightforward, almost brutally so. I liked him immediately.

This straightforward approach, in my mind, would go on to define Bush's presidency. Between Hurricane Katrina, 9/11 and wars in the Persian Gulf, Bush was a controversial president. Some believe he was one of the worst presidents in the history of the U.S. As time goes on, however, I think that history will treat him more kindly.

ON 9/11, I WAS on my way to a second interview at the Pentagon for the position of U.S. assistant secretary of defense. I felt a sense of panic as the plane turned around and rumours spread that the Pentagon and Twin Towers had been hit. People sometimes forget or underestimate the intensity of that terrible time, the flurry of issues and the strong desire for retaliation. When Bush addressed Congress by declaring he would seek revenge, he received a standing ovation. I was 100 percent for the war. It was a knee-jerk reaction, to be sure, but not an outlandish one. There was a chance that Saddam Hussein or his people did have weapons of mass destruction. Chemical weapons had been used in the Iraq/Iran conflict years before. Americans wanted answers quickly, and the Bush administration took two plus two and turned it into five.

It was only when things got tough that Bush's political rivals ducked into their foxholes and went on the counteroffensive. But despite his plunging popularity, the president continued on his chosen course. Whether the world became a better place because of it, I do not know. Bush, however, always acted in character. He did not flinch. I have met too many politicians who act like reeds in the wind. People should look back at Bush and at least view him as consistent.

For better or worse, he guided the U.S. through one of the most difficult and defining moments in its history.

My involvement with the Republican Party increased during the lead-up to the 2000 presidential election. I tried to make myself as visible as possible, including at one high-profile Republican Regent event with George Bush Sr., at the Bush compound in Kennebunkport. The estate was spectacular, jutting out into the Atlantic Ocean on Walker's Point. I remember Bush Sr. zooming into the party on a powerboat, surrounded by the U.S. Coast Guard and Navy SEALS. I still have a picture of the two of us drinking beer together.

Back in Michigan, I threw my support behind Republican nominees. I held parties at our house to raise funds. Once every two weeks, in different parts of the country, I gave platform speeches for Republican candidates. Many of the candidates I supported were re-elected. Some got in for the first time. And of course, George W. Bush became the forty-third president of the U.S. on January 21, 2001.

I was invited to the inauguration that year. I took my eldest daughter, Gemma, because I thought she might benefit from the experience. We had been assigned great seats. In the lead-up to the inauguration there had been a week of parties. Washington lit up with Republican soirees, with dozens of events going on every day. After the inauguration, my daughter and I were invited to a reception along Constitution Avenue. We watched George Bush and his wife, Laura—now President and First Lady—drive past during the victory parade. Later that night, when we returned to our hotel, I changed into my tuxedo and black bow tie. Each state was giving elaborate parties, brimming with food, drinks and entertainment. You could attend them if you knew people. I attended several; the "black tie and boots" Texas party was the highlight. The president stopped in at each party. He looked pumped and elated, shaking hands and laughing before participating in a ceremonial dance. The inauguration was fabulous, to be sure, but it was also a valuable time to campaign and to be seen by fellow Republicans. I made it known that I would be interested in a role in the government once the dust settled. My battles in Detroit had given me a taste for higher-level politics, and of course I was always striving for the next big thing. After I returned to my post at the Detroit Medical Center, it was not long before the phones started ringing.

U.S. political transitions are peaceful, but it is not a friendly process. Clinton had held the White House for eight long years. So when Bush's people took over, Democrats were not waiting on the lawn to shake hands and guide the new guard to their desks. The place was trashed. Employees took all of their files with them. And perhaps most famously, all of the *W*'s were removed from keyboards at the White House. Playtime was over. Republicans were starting from scratch.

To be honest, some members of the party were surprised when Bush won. Not everyone had been expecting it. So the transition team needed to shift into high gear quickly. After any American presidential election, the new administration doles out a few thousand coveted appointments to its friends, some with great salaries and perks, including cabinet positions and ambassadorships. There is something called the Plum Book, so named for its purple cover, that details all of these appointments. After Bush's election, the White House was flooded with calls. The callers reminded staffers how this person and that person had provided favours or contributed generously to the Republican victory. A frenzied job market began. It was time for Bush to reciprocate.

My name was on the list of possible appointees, and I flew up to Washington for an orientation. The White House was vibrating with piss-and-vinegar Republicans who had worked on the campaign. They were mostly white, in their mid-twenties and from somewhere in the Midwest. These were the party zealots, the young and aggressive transition team, who believed in the party doctrine unequivocally. It was their job to make the phone calls and sift through the list of names. It was grunt work. Pulling the strings above them was the older Republican guard. I met with some members of the transition team first. They interviewed me and asked what kind of position I would be interested in.

I had learned very quickly the finer points of American politics. Positions are bought. If you brought in $500,000 or more, through either fundraising or personal contributions to the party, you could be considered for an ambassadorship to somewhere like Finland or Sweden. At $150,000 or less, you would probably end up with a country that ended in "stan," such as Kazakhstan, Tajikistan, Uzbekistan or Kyrgyzstan. How much to become ambassador of Sweden? Big-time Republicans could stroll into the office and ask that.

The approach is totally un-Canadian. In American politics, it is easier to get a seat at the table than it is in Canada, if you know the rules. In Canada, you must be extremely well known if you want to play. Being brash and aggressive does not count. You need recommendations. In the U.S., it can be an expensive proposition getting involved in politics, especially if you do not have family connections. The political machine is larger and more complex, and as a result it must be oiled frequently to run well.

The cycle of power for many American political positions lasts only two years. While the president appoints people to cabinet posts, with ratification by the Senate, there are a host of elected positions as well, such as sheriffs and judges. Those with political aspirations are constantly trolling the population and campaigning for the next election, making sure they can secure financial backing and contributions. The latter are particularly important.

After my interview with White House staffers, I found myself sitting in front of Tommy Thompson, former governor of Wisconsin, who had been selected as Bush's secretary of health. Thompson got right to the point: I was being considered as assistant secretary of health, the number two position in the country when it comes to healthcare. I told him that I would be very interested, but I was even more interested in the surgeon general position. As I had learned with the board of directors at the Detroit Medical Center, being direct, forceful and confident about expressing your desires can pay off.

The surgeon general was a term position, and one not necessarily under the president's control. David Satcher held the post, and he still had another year to go in his term. Thompson and I considered the possibility of my taking the assistant secretary of health job in the interim, although in truth, Republicans simply wanted Satcher to resign. It was unclear whether that could be made to happen.

No decisions were made that day, and shortly after returning to Detroit I received another call. This time, it was the Department of Defense inviting me down to the Pentagon to interview for the position of assistant secretary of defense. The offer surprised me in the beginning. What did I know about defense? In essence, however, the Department of Defense was simply a huge business involving more than one million people. The department had three secretaries, one each for logistics, military and human resources. I was being considered for the latter.

TWO SERGEANTS MET me at the entrance to the Pentagon, and they did not leave my side for an instant. I was escorted into the bowels of the facility. When we reached our destination, I saw a sign on the table that read: "This room has been cleared for secrets."

It was an exciting time, but really only one position intrigued me, and it soon became clear that surgeon general was indeed within my grasp. After coming by my office at the Detroit Medical Center, the Secret Service wanted to visit my home. I left work early to meet them at the door as my children came home from school. Two agents entered the house and looked around, asking my family questions in the same official and respectful manner as before. Then I took the agents on a tour. They stuck their heads into each room and peeked at the photos on the walls.

At this stage, I think the Secret Service was simply looking for red flags, such as drugs on the kitchen table or illegal immigrants working as housemaids. It felt like they were ticking off items on a checklist. The agents also interviewed some of our neighbours, ensuring I was a standup citizen who did not engage in suspicious activities or host wild parties. To some, the whole process might seem intrusive or daunting. Most people are not accustomed to having their lives put under a microscope. However, I felt surprisingly relaxed throughout the process. After all, the government had approached me. I did not feel a great deal of pressure, though in a way, the reality had not yet hit home. On some level, I never thought the appointment would actually happen, so this was a flattering and interesting exercise. I found myself looking up the surgeon general's uniform online. It was awfully impressive, with its braids and hardware. I was fascinated with just the idea of becoming surgeon general.

I did get nervous, however, when the phone starting ringing with calls from the media. By now, word had got out that I was a front-runner. Articles started to appear in the local newspaper. Some people worried that I would be leaving the Detroit Medical Center. Others were surprised, saying they had had no idea I was a Republican and so politically driven and well connected. I even got calls from strangers, Republicans from across the country who insisted they had ideas for healthcare. All kinds of people started hitching themselves to my wagon. It got awfully heavy. Suddenly the possibility was glaringly real, and the time had come to ask my family and myself some hard questions.

We had a family meeting around the kitchen table. This job was not just about me. I knew it would profoundly impact my wife and children. Our lives would change. Pamela had never been keen on a public life. She did not relish the cocktail parties, the schmoozing or playing the political game. The children would have to be escorted to school by Marines. I would not be able to travel outside of the U.S. without permission, and I would have to give up my various business interests. All of these factors were strikes against the job. But most importantly, as surgeon general I would have to be a party worker, an employee of the Republican Party. As such, I would be at the beck and call of others.

It is better knowing the king than being the king, I reminded myself. I enjoyed serving as an advisor and influencer. Political power had its restrictions. It was a difficult decision to make, but when the job was offered, I turned it down. I disappointed some people in government, particularly my supporters. My decision was even enough to warrant a phone call from President Bush.

"Arthur, I heard you turned down the offer from the secretary of health," he said.

"That's right, Mr. President."

He paused for a brief moment, then said, "Final answer?"

The question made me laugh. Bush was referencing that famous line from the TV game show *Who Wants to Be a Millionaire?* I was honoured that the president thought to call me. He was giving me one last chance to reconsider. But my mind was made up.

"Final answer," I stated evenly.

Bush was not the only one to call me. A whole range of people had anticipated some kind of benefit or elevation if my appointment came to fruition. Two supporters in the Senate had also lined up in preparation for my hearing and confirmation—Trent Lott of Mississippi and Judd Gregg from New Hampshire.

Serving as U.S. surgeon general would have been a unique opportunity. The attack to come on September 11 and the ensuing wars would have made the job even more interesting. Usually the surgeon general tells people not to smoke, to keep fit and to wear a condom. I could have brought something special to the position in a crisis. It was not my personality to fade into the background, and perhaps I could have shaped healthcare during those difficult times.

INSTEAD, I GOT the chance to do that in a different way. A few weeks after I turned down the job, Bush offered me a spot on the Presidential Commission tasked with reviewing healthcare at the Department of Defense and the Veterans Administration. The subject interested me, and the position would last only two years, without the baggage that came with other positions. In addition, one year later, Michigan's Governor Engler appointed me chairman of Michigan's Hospital Commission. So I stayed in the political game without cashing in all of my chips.

At the Department of Defense, we discussed the delivery of healthcare in battlefield situations—Afghanistan, for example—and transporting sick or injured members of the military to U.S. facilities in Europe before returning them to home soil.

The Veterans Administration faced a more pressing concern. During the election campaign, Bush had pledged to re-examine the delivery of care for military veterans. The system, completely subsidized by the Department of Defense, had become increasingly sluggish and financially strapped. Veterans were complaining about quality of care and long wait times, grievances not unlike the issues in Canada's healthcare system. I made the argument that the government should get out of the business of healthcare entirely. Some two thousand veterans' hospitals existed in the country. They employed thousands of doctors and nurses. However, delivering and funding the service represented two strongly opposed interests. The delivery side wanted more drugs, hospitals and beds. The financial side wanted to restrict those additions and save money. I urged the government to provide only the financing. Should we not just give them all a healthcare card and let them choose where they wanted to be treated? It was a difficult issue, partly because the delivery of care was so well established. But I think the message got out. There has been more integration with the mainstream healthcare system in recent years, especially through partnerships, when it comes to complex procedures.

I remained a strong Republican until I left Detroit in 2003. Over the years that followed, I would watch as the party deteriorated and the Democrats rose to prominence. Although I have never met Barack Obama, some of my American friends have commented that I would probably get along better with Obama than I did with Bush. I find that surprising. It is as if my African roots, and the fact that Obama is black, should necessitate a strong relationship between us. People forget that Abraham Lincoln, the man who freed the slaves, was a Republican. I respect Obama. I think it's terrific that the U.S. demonstrated that someone from a minority group could take on the highest office in the land. But like I always say, you must remain consistent politically. Never change your flag.

Despite my support for the Republicans, however, I was glad when Obama won a second term. He deserved it, mostly because the Republicans put up such a lousy candidate. I found it incredible that Mitt Romney continuously appealed to such a narrow base: the white, wealthy and successful business community. Romney missed a huge opportunity in the selection of his running mate. He could have chosen a Hispanic woman, for example. Instead, he chose a "Mini-Me," someone who reflected his own background and values.

I believe that the Republican campaign got increasingly xenophobic, and only after the fact did Romney's team realize why they had lost. It was not so much Romney who dropped the ball as those around him. But the loss may have galvanized the party.

A few of my principles made me an unusual Republican Party member. I believed in a woman's right to choose. I was a supporter of stem cell research. And I was more liberal than most Republicans in my opinions concerning immigration. It was on these points that I experienced tension with right-wing members. Some of the politicians I butted heads with would go on to form the Tea Party, a group I will never understand. It goes without saying that its members are not well endowed with neurons. The U.S. government shutdown in 2013 would only confirm that fact. I think the Republican Party will have difficulty reconciling the Tea Party's radical theories with what is needed to govern. Over time, the movement will likely fade and go the way of the religious right. At the end of the day, moderate Democrats and Republicans will rule the U.S. In the near future, I think the party will learn to modernize and bridge these ideological gaps.

While I struggled with the Republican Party's rigid social policies, I liked small government. I owned guns. I allied myself with the economic views of Republicans. As I would discover, my political views actually placed me more in line with the Conservative Party of Canada. That would soon prove fortuitous.

BACK IN THE Bahamas in 2003, following my resignation from the Detroit Medical Center, my phone started ringing.

I was invited to consider becoming the head of SUNY Down-state Medical Center in Brooklyn. I was asked to run a major hospital network in Georgia. I also got an offer to take over one of the largest public hospital networks in the state of California.

And then Montreal, Canada, came calling. They were looking for a "ball-buster" to accomplish what nobody else had been able to do for more than a decade. It was exactly the challenge I was looking for.

6.

A MAN OF
MANY HATS

TONY DAGNONE AND I were not on speaking terms. Yet there we were, practically side by side at the 2006 Shriners Annual Convention in Baltimore, Maryland. I was now the CEO of the McGill University Health Centre, a position I had accepted in February 2004, and he was president and CEO of the London Health Sciences Centre. Between us, thousands of Shriners were streaming into the giant auditorium, and Dagnone and I were making last-second pitches for votes, handing out pamphlets and shaking hands. In a few minutes, these delegates from across North America would decide the location of the Shriners Children's Hospital. Would it be Montreal, where the original Shriners Hospital had been situated for over one hundred years, or would it relocate to London? Ontario or Quebec? French or English? Nearly two years of intense lobbying had come down to this moment. This vote was about more than just a hospital.

I had been brought to Montreal to help build a $1.3-billion mega-hospital. But keeping the Shriners Hospital in Quebec and out of Ontario would prove to be a crash course in Quebec politics. It would also be a prelude to bigger battles I would face—political, cultural and personal—over the mega-hospital.

I HAD BARELY begun at the McGill University Health Centre when I got a call from the Shriners, letting me know that the leadership was strongly considering moving the hospital to London, Ontario. The Shriners Hospital was a specialized institution, treating patients, mostly with bone and joint problems, from across Canada as well as from the northeastern U.S. It had only fifty or sixty beds, and much of its work was done on an outpatient basis. But a coveted research centre was attached to the hospital.

Although it was a courtesy call and no formal decision had been made, it seemed pretty clear to me that their minds were already made up.

Moving a hospital from one province to another was not typical, especially one that had been in Montreal for more than a century. But the hospital looked its age. And although there had been talk about building a new facility for quite some time, nobody expected that it could be built anywhere other than Montreal. I quickly learned that the Shriners' relationship with Quebec had, like the hospital, also deteriorated. The Shriners had recently met with provincial leaders, and they were less than pleased with the reception. Communication was poor. Despite a long history, the Shriners no longer felt appreciated in Quebec. The government did not care for them much either. The Shriners' leadership, hailing from the American South, did not always take well to French Canadians. It might be an international organization, but at its core the Shriners is led by white, affluent American Republicans with fairly right-wing views. The hospital had been built during a time of anglophone dominance. René Lévesque Boulevard had been Dorcester Boulevard. In the twenty-first century, Montreal, now liberal and French, seemed more like foreign territory to the Shriners.

London, on the other hand, had stepped up to the plate, wining and dining the Shriners. Attractive plans and incentives for the new hospital had been laid at their feet.

From a medical point of view, losing the hospital would be a blow. As far as Quebec's leadership was concerned, however, the departure of the Shriners Hospital, politically speaking, would be a slap in the face: the Americans judging London as superior to Quebec and the English as superior to the French.

Although it seemed obvious to me that we had already lost, I saw it as a real opportunity to do battle, to not simply lie down and die. In 2004, I was fresh off the boat, full of energy and fight. If we lost, the loss would be historical, not personal. These issues existed long before my arrival in Montreal, and I felt no deep investment in them. But if we won, if I could turn it around, what a victory it would be for the McGill University Health Centre.

So began my first political campaign in Canada. I made it clear to the Shriners that, win or lose, Montreal would not give up so easily. There would be a bidding process and a vote.

My first step was to attend the Shriners Annual Convention in Denver, Colorado, in 2005. Face time was important. The Shriners needed to know not only that they were wanted in Quebec, but also that new leadership at the McGill University Health Centre was sympathetic to their interests. I did not expect a resolution in Denver. The

Shriners simply said that they would keep an open mind and make a final decision at the next general meeting, in Baltimore. That gave both Montreal and London a chance to campaign in earnest.

And boy, oh boy, did the mud start to fly. London issued a statement claiming that Montreal's proposed site for the new Shriners Hospital wing was a dump, and thus contaminated and unfit for children. They made it sound as though patients would morph into little monsters and mutants. How can you build a hospital, especially one for children, on a dump? Those accusations were partly true. The forty-two-acre site of the new mega-hospital was an old railway yard and city dump. Of course, elaborate plans had been made to excavate and sanitize the entire area. I hired someone from the U.S. to do an inspection, and it was declared safe. Bringing in an American inspector, in addition to a Canadian, had been my idea. I wanted the Shriners to feel as comfortable and involved with the process as possible. In the lead-up to Baltimore, I also spent a lot of time with the Shriner leadership. We invited them to Montreal and schmoozed them to death, making them feel at home and hoping it would be enough to sweeten the sour taste in their mouths.

The rest of that year was one big auction. In addition to financial incentives and tax breaks, London offered to build a ten-storey tower beside the Children's Hospital of Western Ontario, with a bridge connecting the two structures. The Shriners asked if we could do better. I ran around Montreal, holding meetings with the premier, the health minister and the board of directors. We decided to offer them a full five acres and similar financial incentives. The Shriners had the option to join with the new mega-hospital or maintain their independence. Next was a debate over naming rights: the Shriners wanted to be part of the mega-hospital, but at the same time maintain a degree of sovereignty. Meanwhile, they were having the same conversation in London. It was a constant back-and-forth and one-upmanship. Rumours started to fly that back-door deals had been struck between hospital executives in London and senior Shriners, although none of those claims were substantiated.

Prior to the convention, Premier Jean Charest, Health Minister Philippe Couillard and I had met privately to discuss the "what if." If the Shriners chose to leave Montreal, it would be crushing. How would we respond? What was never made public was that Charest had authorized the building of the Quebec Orthopedic Centre on the mega-hospital site, a $110-million addition to the $1.3-billion plan. Its services would mimic those offered at the Shriners Hospital. We had no idea where the money would come from. All we knew was that we had to announce something. Some preliminary designs had already been commissioned. If we lost in our bid, we would call a press conference and hold up a fancy rendering for the media.

WHEN WE ARRIVED in Baltimore, Charest, Couillard, Montreal Mayor Gérald Tremblay and I booked a suite and set up a model of the new hospital. The Ontario team—Dagnone, Premier Dalton McGuinty, Health Minister George Smitherman and London Mayor Anne Marie DeCicco-Best—did the same.

Both Quebec and Ontario had brought out the big guns, and both sides came out firing. At the opening ceremony, before the speeches started, our respective delegations came face to face for the first time. In a room buzzing with people, McGuinty and Charest shook hands and smiled, though it did not take long before tempers flared.

"Why are you taking this hospital from us?" Charest asked pointedly.

"Taking?" McGuinty laughed, releasing his hand crisply. "Montreal had the Shriners Hospital for a hundred years. Your time is up."

That was when things got ugly. You could sense the mercury rising in the room. I heard the exchange and moved to Charest's side in support. Couillard and Tremblay followed suit.

Charest appeared flustered. "If the hospital goes, it could lead to other problems between us. What you are doing is damaging," Charest boomed. He was not screaming, but it was close.

By now McGuinty's gang had also noticed the scuffle. With entourages on each side, pride was on the line. Neither side wanted to lose face.

"Look, Ontario has a legitimate bid. It's a free country, Jean. And the fact is, a Shriners Hospital in Ontario would service far more people. It makes more sense," McGuinty shot back. "Our bid is better for Canadians."

Charest scowled. "I want you to know that this won't be the last of it," he replied, seething, but calmly running both hands down his suit.

The premiers retreated into their corners with delegations in tow. It was the first and last exchange on the matter at the convention.

Throughout the convention, I made a point of dropping in on as many Shriners from different states and provinces as possible. Quebec was seen as the underdog. Some believed it was a case of too little, too late. The London bid was too far ahead. The Shriners had already moved on psychologically from Montreal. Plus the Shriners had a much stronger tradition in Ontario. Far more Ontario Shriners were at the convention, and they were far more influential than those representing Montreal. Quebec's largest city only had one Shriners lodge. And as I watched the last of the Shriners trickle into that auditorium, hundreds of tassels swaying on little red hats, I saw Dagnone, my counterpart in London, smiling across at me through the crowd. It was the first time we had really looked at each other since that altercation at the start of the convention.

When the doors closed, he walked over and extended his hand.

"Job well done, Arthur," he said. "You all put up a good fight. But I have a feeling that Ontario is going to win this one."

"Thank you, Tony. Now, if you will excuse me," I replied, turning towards the chair beside me. Resting there was a tall, black hatbox. I opened it, lifted out the red velvet fez with its long black tassel and the word KARNAK emblazoned on its front, signifying Montreal's sole Shriner lodge, and placed it on my head.

"I need to go inside and vote."

I did not stay to see the look on his face, although I now wish I had. I strode crisply for the double doors and opened them with both hands.

As a thirty-second-degree Freemason, I had already been well on my way towards Shriners membership. In the year between the conventions in Denver and Baltimore, I had completed my initiation. Throughout the convention in Baltimore, I wore my Shriners hat and attended events reserved exclusively for members. I had access to the leadership in

ways the Ontario delegation did not. Word spread that the
CEO representing the Montreal bid was on the level. A few
days before the convention, I had even marched in the Shriner parade, side by side with my brothers. Pound for pound,
I knew Montreal would probably lose. Becoming a Shriner
was my ace in the hole.

In the end, each side was given a chance to make final
remarks. I had carefully prepped our representative. He
made a joke, pointing out that Baltimore was actually built
on a dump. The crowd roared with laughter.

We won by a landslide. Whether my membership was a
factor or not, wrenching the hospital back into Quebec's
hands was a huge win for Montreal. And much of the praise
was heaped upon me. It was a defining moment in my
Canadian career. The campaign I had launched bridged the
gaps between business, medicine and politics. It verified to
many people why I had been brought to Montreal in the
first place: I got things done.

With the hard-fought Shriners Hospital battle won, it
was perhaps no surprise that opportunities in both business
and politics soon started to present themselves.

I FOUND MYSELF on Quebec's side by professional necessity.
But it was obvious to everyone around me where I stood
politically. I had a few wardrobe malfunctions at first. In
the U.S., I always wore a red bow tie to signify my Republican allegiance. Of course, in Canada, red is the colour
of the Liberals, bitter rivals to the Conservatives, and that
would not do at all. Getting dressed each morning, I caught
myself more than once in the mirror before walking out the
door, prompting me to run upstairs and swap my red bow
tie for the Tory blue.

The political landscape had changed since the last time I was in Canada. In the late 1980s, the Liberals ruled. But now, nearly twenty years later, the party was in a semi-state of collapse. They were not the same Liberals from the Trudeau or Chrétien years. Their established order was getting older. Young blood was in short supply. While the Conservatives held a minority government, and the team was relatively inexperienced, they were a force to be reckoned with. I had developed strong relationships with leading Conservatives in Alberta many years before, and in some respects I considered the party Republican Lite. I suppose some Tories in Alberta and elsewhere had far-right-wing policies. Generally speaking, however, I slipped into the Tory doctrine quite effortlessly.

Of course, Canada will always be a Liberal country. Every election is the Liberals' to lose. In recent years, the party has continued to build momentum with its young blood, most notably through Justin Trudeau, son of the legendary prime minister Pierre Trudeau. The strategy makes sense. He does have name recognition. He has charisma. Elections in the twenty-first century are won and lost on television and media. It is all about how you look, as opposed to how bright you are. We're in the era of the ten-second sound bite. And if you can perfect that sound, even for a split second, the substance becomes secondary. The Liberals have a very good shot at regaining the country's leadership. The New Democratic Party has made admirable strides of late as the only true left-wing party. Whether it can ever truly cast off its identity as the third party in Canada, however, is highly debatable. Bob Rae was the leader of the NDP when they ruled Ontario in the early 1990s, but in the end he returned to the Liberals, where the bread is buttered. The NDP is too left-wing, closer to the Green Party, and notwithstanding periodic surges in support, as when Jack Layton ran the party, it will always be sitting on the fringes of Canadian politics.

The Bloc Québécois is also on the fringes. In truth, I've never understood how the Bloc was given full national status while running on a separatist agenda and fielding candidates in only one province. Can you imagine a separatist party that ran candidates only in Manitoba? Or British Columbia? Nevertheless, Bloc Québécois members receive a paycheque from the federal government with a little Canadian flag in the corner. I'm sure they cash it.

I supported Montreal causes, but I never let an isolationist or separatist agenda govern my approach. As in Detroit, I had access to decision makers. Most hospital administrators do not use their job to parlay themselves onto the national stage. I felt, however, that as the head of an English-speaking hospital in Quebec, I had the opportunity to raise the hospital's profile, as well as my own.

Being different and working outside of Quebec helped us get noticed.

In many respects, Quebec was a closed box. It was a mini-country in itself. Every national organization or research council had a provincial equivalent, and indeed it was frowned upon to venture outside. For example, the Fonds de recherche du Québec-Santé was similar to the Canada Foundation for Innovation and the Canadian Institutes of Health Research. While I applied to the Quebec organizations, I started developing relationships outside of the province as well. I think that it actually gave us an advantage. We did the unexpected. Perhaps that was why we were awarded nearly $100 million from the Canadian Foundation for Innovation for the research centre, the largest grant in its history. It was later matched by the Quebec government and supported by donors, bringing the grand total up to $250 million. It also put me in contact with leaders of the day.

Tony Clement, Canada's minister of health, was a close friend and ally throughout my time at the McGill University Health Centre. In turn, I attended his events in Quebec, saying nice things and making him look good. He was a true Tory, down to the bones, and through him I met others in the party. As I had done in Detroit with the Republicans, I cultivated a keen sense of loyalty. I always gave the maximum party contribution each year. I attended fundraisers for local and national candidates, even for those I knew would never win. Once you meet people professionally, you become close socially. You become friends.

I made a point of going to Ottawa every second or third week for a day or two, and in the evenings I would have a drink or two at Hy's Steakhouse, a well-known haunt for the Conservative brain trust. I rapidly became known, and within a year of assuming my position, I found myself at a Conservative cocktail party at the War Museum in Ottawa, face to face with Prime Minister Stephen Harper.

THE RECEPTION WAS held in the museum's atrium. Tanks, personnel carriers and fighter planes surrounded us as the crowd formed an orderly line, waiting their turn to shake Harper's hand. Our first encounter was brief, given the circumstances. We exchanged a few pleasantries. He asked about the mega-hospital and I gave an update on our progress. As it turned out, that conversation was a fairly typical exchange. The prime minister was not a man of many words. Harper resembled an accountant or economist, which I suppose he was, rather than the archetypal leader of a nation. He was not expansive, gregarious or charismatic. When he first came into office, his team enrolled him in smiling classes, simply because he was too straight and serious during speeches or when interacting with the public.

The Conservatives were the right party at the right time. Harper was successful because he was a strategic thinker. He understood the economics of Canada. He was also wise in his appointments, so he was able to structure the country in such a way that it could prosper or at least hold the line following the crash of 2008. Compared to the U.S. and Europe, Canada became a bastion of stability, and the Conservatives deserve a great deal of credit.

My exposure to Harper would increase over the coming years. I saw him in Ottawa every so often through structured meetings, and very occasionally one on one. I convinced him to visit the McGill University Health Centre, and it was the first time a prime minister had done so. But most of the time, our association was indirect. Harper did not hold meetings unless they were necessary. That was his style. I heard through others that he was supportive. I did not bother him, and I think he appreciated that.

It became very clear to me that the way to Harper's heart was through the party. In my view, he put party first, country second. If you told him that you had an idea to help Canada, he might thank you and you'd get invited back for a meeting in five years. If you had a strategy for boosting the party's profile and polling numbers, step right inside. I was a party man myself, so I could relate well to his approach.

ANOTHER VALUABLE opportunity arose when I met Robert Milton. He and I had crossed paths at various social events in Montreal. He was not only the head of Air Canada, the country's flag carrier, but also chairman, president and CEO of its parent company, ACE Aviation Holdings. In 2003, Air Canada filed for bankruptcy, and he led them through a restructuring. While the airline had been saved, its future was unclear. It had been privatized in the late 1980s, but in many respects it still hauled the anchor of a public sector enterprise.

Air Canada was a bilingual business, imposing strict stipulations on staff as if it were a government department. Therefore, if you wanted to be cabin crew but you were from Alberta and did not speak French, you were probably out of luck. The fact that most Canadians outside of Quebec do not speak French fluently was painfully brought to the fore, bringing with it major financial implications. It was a human resources nightmare. You could not hire adequate staff in western Canada and expect them all to speak the language. It made the distribution of staff very difficult, creating huge costs in terms of training, and generally placed the airline at a competitive disadvantage.

Linked with language issues was Air Canada's head office, located in Montreal. Under the terms of privatization, Quebec had insisted that the headquarters stay put. Moving it elsewhere was considered a deal breaker. The office represented some one thousand jobs, many of which were the most senior positions at Air Canada. And as with the prospect of the Shriners Hospital leaving for London, pride was involved. The number of national corporations headquartered in the province had dwindled over the years.

Another disadvantage was the airline's obligation to fly to every provincial capital daily. From its days as a Crown corporation, this protocol was considered paramount if Air Canada wanted to knit the country together and call itself a national flag carrier. Of course, it did not always make economic sense. For example, direct flights year-round to Charlottetown, the capital of Prince Edward Island, were not the biggest driver of revenue.

The biggest problem, however, was Air Canada's pension plan. By all accounts, it was off the charts. As with any other government job, the base pay was not glamorous. But it offered top-notch benefits, great job security and a comfy pension once retirement rolled around. Representing some $3 billion in liabilities, the plan had been built up over twenty-five years. It was easily more than double that of any competitor in North America. Obsolete and inflated, it reminded me of the automotive industry in Detroit. The company could no longer sustain the program while keeping its head above water, let alone turning a profit. WestJet, headquartered in Calgary, Alberta, had become a serious competitor in recent years. This airline was completely private and not held back by language rules, imposed route schedules or a plump pension plan.

Milton and I met for lunch several times, often discussing these issues. He felt that I had something to offer the board of directors, and sure enough, I was sworn in at Air Canada's annual general meeting in 2006.

Our job was to advise the airline's management on how to negotiate with government. The Harper administration knew that Air Canada needed to cut the public-sector cord. It was just a matter of how and when. Air Canada was a major employer. The workers had grown accustomed to sucking at the government's teat, and cutting them off abruptly would not go over well during the next political election.

It was a constant back-and-forth—making concessions here, trimming back there—in an effort to get all sides focused on reality. The fact was, we had allowed the public sector to carry this burden for far too long. It was like we were swimming in a pool with Etihad, Qatar Airways, American Airlines and Southwest, but while they slipped on flippers, Air Canada strapped on boots. The pension was, of course, the biggest nut to crack. Back then, nobody could believe it was the primary source of Air Canada's financial woes—or perhaps nobody wanted to believe it. There must be other ways to save money, they thought. Denial was rampant.

In 2006 and beyond, I do not think people realized just how close the airline came to filing for bankruptcy. The board had already discussed the possibility with lawyers and accountants. Plans were in place. The financial difficulties reached their peak in 2009. After suffering a $400-million loss in the first quarter, Air Canada appealed for a moratorium on pension payments. The airline was within a week of folding. Government and airline executives held round-the-clock negotiations. If the airline could not pay its pension obligations, it would default on just about everything, including the fuel bill. The ripple effect would be disastrous.

The airline was saved once more. Part of the strategy was to hire new workers under Air Canada's subsidiary airlines, such as Rouge. These planes tended to perform the short, low-volume routes, and because it was a separate company, employees could be hired under more realistic terms. In other words, the airline would wean itself off the pension plan, grandfathering it out over a generation. And in so doing, it made progress in drifting away from its public-sector legacy.

Progress was also made on improving route schedules and loosening French-language requirements. These changes were made not as a result of tension, but because of economic realities. Arguments to maintain the status quo did not hold much water.

Unfortunately, they had to be tackled with time and kid gloves. Some things will probably never change, like the headquarters in Montreal, even though senior leadership in my day wanted it in Toronto. If a solution could not be reached, you worked around it—phasing out the pension plan with subsidiaries, or shifting practical responsibilities to the Toronto office but keeping the symbolic headquarters in Montreal. It was politics and business, business and politics, and one could not be separated from the other.

Management continuously worked with government, either directly or indirectly. When I met people in government, Air Canada would inevitably come up as a point of discussion. Combined with the McGill University Health Centre and a number of other interests, my time at Air Canada was simply another springboard for reaching the greater political heights to come.

AMIDST ALL THIS, someone at the federal level approached me about the prospect of taking over the healthcare portfolio. I was asked to find a seat to run in.

Quebec was not an option, because you had to speak French, even if you lived in Westmount. People would attack you for that weakness. It came up, however, that I used to live in Alberta when I first started my medical career. They could arrange for a safe seat. After all, nearly every seat in Alberta is safe for the Conservatives.

No, Alberta was too damn cold. And my father would never approve. Kidding aside, I did not seek political office for the same reasons I had withdrawn from the surgeon general race. I had too many other business interests. I wanted to be free to operate. And most importantly, I had a mega-hospital on my plate.

7.

THE HOSPITAL THAT PORTER BUILT

MONTREAL'S MCGILL UNIVERSITY Health Centre was considered an anglophone bastion, a Goliath of English language and tradition, and many Quebecers were constantly flinging stones at it. I used to tell people that McGill University was first in Canada but second in Quebec. It was easily one of Canada's finest institutions, yet its bilingualism was not enough to appease a great number of Quebecers. McGill was the red-haired stepchild. Canada was the dysfunctional parent. And the province of Quebec was the rebellious, dissatisfied teenager still trying to discover itself in the world.

Quebec should have separated from Canada following its second referendum on the matter in 1995. The vote had been close, with 49 percent in favour of separation. Since then, discontent had continued to fester. Quebec carried on like an adolescent girl stomping her heels. She wanted to do something, but mommy and daddy would not let her. This desire for independence manifested itself in all the wrong ways. Many signs in the province could be printed only in French, and in no other language. Let us call it *hambourgeois*, not *hamburger*. An Italian restaurant in Quebec was even ordered to remove the word *pasta* from its menu because it was considered too ethnic and not "French." Once I was hired, my secretary was required to say *allô* or *bonjour* before *hello* when she picked up the phone. In Quebec, the French lacked the power they wanted, so they fretted about the small stuff. If the sovereigntists had won the referendum, Quebec could have become a country in its own right. It would have grown to become an adult, capable of adult conversations.

As with the fight over the Shriners Hospital, the building of McGill's super-hospital was a microcosm of a much larger issue in Canada. In some respects, the process felt more like a complex sociological experiment than a business transaction.

When the McGill University Health Centre first called me in 2004, they had been trying and failing for more than a decade to build their new hospital. Running alongside their plans, but with equal ineptitude, was another mega-project mounted through the University of Montreal. The huge difference was that the University of Montreal medical facility, if successful, would be exclusively French. As it was, neither project could get off the ground. The politics and the linguistic tensions in Quebec never stopped swirling, leaving the issues of the day frozen in place.

Some people were in favour of combining the two projects. While the theory made sense, there was already too much baggage to make that practical. A united hospital might also have received support from the French community, but some considered such a proposition an affront to

McGill. The English establishment feared that once a joint mega-hospital was built, the French would simply take over. It was an odd state of affairs. Everyone seemed to be in the same boat. We were all Canadians. And yet we were clearly divided. My mandate was to make the English hospital happen.

The McGill board had hired me for the aggressive, no-holds-barred approach I'd demonstrated in Detroit. Even though I had been an outsider there, I had played politics, stood up to the establishment and prevailed. On my first day in Montreal, I was presented with enough reports, plans and designs to fill an entire room. The board had gone through several administrators, but nobody seemed to get the job done. What they needed was someone different, someone not afraid to go in for the kill.

In Detroit, I had fired thousands of people with the stroke of a pen. In Canada, though, nobody has the same cutthroat mentality. Let's not fire people now, they say. Let's retain them to do other things, look at attrition and when employees are sixty-five, escort them quietly out the door. Some might say this approach is very Canadian. In my opinion, it was not generally Canadian so much as indicative of hospital administrators in the country. I brought a radically different approach to the Quebec healthcare scene.

At first, I thought returning to Canada would be a homecoming. But this was not Alberta. I might as well have been dropped into a foreign country. Montreal, with all its differences in language, politics and culture, was not accessible to my wife and family. They stayed in Nassau. Since I was in the city alone, I didn't live in Montreal seven days a week—I kept a place there but left on weekends for the Bahamas. I ran my cancer clinic and saw patients in Montreal, but the

Bahamas was home. My children went to school there and had friends. I had considered bringing them to Quebec initially, but the province's laws quickly changed my mind. Since my daughters had never attended school in Canada, they would have been forced to attend a French-speaking institution. They were teenagers and did not speak a lick of it. These kinds of language laws and linguistic racism never let me feel entirely at home in Quebec.

So on a personal level, taking the job in Montreal was hard. In Detroit, my family and I had lived far outside the city, and while I tended to work crazy hours downtown, at least we were together in the same country. It bothered me that now I could not spend much time with my wife and children. I sometimes failed to properly calculate the timing on milestones such as birthdays, anniversaries and graduations, especially as plans for the new super-hospital really started to heat up. I had more than one of those "I don't understand" moments with Pamela, and perhaps with the kids. At the end of each day, I was tired, and I lacked the energy even to speak on the phone and explain my job to my wife. Montreal was my reality, not hers. To her, it felt like she was asking: What did you do yesterday on the moon? As for me, where could I begin? The space between us felt vast.

It was a lonely time, and Montreal's famous parties and social life only made that feeling worse. My position continually necessitated appearances at events and soirees like the Red Cross Ball and the Canadian Cancer Society's gala. I would purposely show up at the beginning of the cocktail hour, making sure everyone knew I was there. I did the rounds and chatted with a few key people. But when the dinner bell rang and couples began to head to their tables, arm in arm, I would slip out the front door. I was embarrassed that there would be an empty seat beside me at the table. I suppose, in some way, that seat represented my isolation in Montreal. I usually enjoyed socializing, dining and dancing, but in general I did not partake of the Montreal social scene.

I did host parties from time to time, organized by my secretary and put on at my penthouse apartment on Doctor Penfield Avenue. I was with people constantly through my work, and as tends to happen, I would often hear the phrases "let's have a drink soon" and "we simply must get together." They were often empty words, of course, but it behooved me to meet with twenty or thirty "obligatories," as I liked to call them, from time to time. We would have a drink or two, perhaps something to eat, and fulfill social conventions.

I had arrived in the city as somewhat of a misfit and a curiosity. People knew I had come from Detroit. Was I American? Yet I had worked in Alberta and Ontario. So I must be Canadian. But I also held a diplomatic passport from Sierra Leone. I was a wild card, with an approach the board of directors at the McGill University Health Centre was not accustomed to. It was a position I felt comfortable with by now.

I did not disappoint them. I did my homework before our first meeting. By speaking with fellow executives, I learned that the chairman of the board typically sat at the head of the boardroom table. He led the meeting and simply asked the hospital staff questions. I knew this arrangement would not work for me at all. So I came in early the morning of the meeting and slid a second chair alongside the first one at the head of the table. There I sat, smiling in my bow tie, fingers linked on the table in front of me, as the board filed in. They represented the icons of business in Montreal, mostly anglophone, although they had held little power since the so-called Quiet Revolution of the 1960s. French families had gradually eroded anglophone corporate and political influence. Many of the big English banks and institutions had uprooted and headed for Toronto. But these anglophones were still prominent members of the community. They had good names.

Not one of them, however, was quite sure how to react to my game of musical chairs. It was somewhat of an emperor's clothing scenario. One of the biggest differences between Canada and the U.S. is that Americans will tell you exactly what they are thinking, especially when it comes to business. I got a few looks from board members that day. I knew what they were thinking. And yet we all let it slide.

At our second meeting, I understood, something would need to be said. I arrived early once more. This time, I left only one chair at the head of that table, and I sat in it myself. I had instructed all of my staff to stay home. Once the board members had taken their seats, I explained to them that I would be running the meeting. They were used to having other hospital executives at meetings for questioning as well. From now on, I told them, they would deal with only one employee—me. The other fourteen thousand people at McGill University Health Centre were my employees. If the board wanted to speak with my employees, they could do so through me. If they did not like what was happening, they could always fire me. I also requested—perhaps demanded— that my title be amended to include CEO. "Director general" never did feel right on its own. I was not the leader of the Salvation Army.

It is in my personality to take over. I was never one to take a back seat. Beyond that, I was living up to expectations. I was brought to Montreal for a reason, to take control and get things done, although the reality turned out to be far more complicated. In keeping with the English and French tension in Quebec, there was a divided mindset towards the mega-hospital. It was clear that the city was of two minds. One side of the brain kept saying yes, while the other said no, which is presumably why nothing had happened for so many years.

I got the sense that the board was relieved I had arrived. But in private corners, there was panic that change was coming. Charest and Couillard epitomized this division.

Couillard, known by some in politics as "the Bear," was about six feet tall, with a very striking face, bright blue eyes and a fuzzy white beard. Of course, I never called him the Bear; to me, he was always Philippe. My close relationship with him in particular would be well documented by the media.

While it's true that we had a very close personal relationship, I remember our first meeting was rather uneventful. When I was first interviewed for the job, I stopped by his office and we shook hands and had a very official kind of conversation. Even after I was appointed, I was pretty guarded in my discussions with him. In the beginning, you want to listen more than you speak. It was very clear to me, however, that he was very important when it came to healthcare in Quebec. And it was equally clear that the anglophone hospital administrators had not played a very good political game. Prior to my arrival, a swagger, a tone of arrogance, characterized their dealings with the provincial government. They did what they wanted. So my tenure would be defined by extending the olive branch. From there, a friendship grew between us.

Couillard and I were similar in some respects. He was a fairly accomplished neurosurgeon, and we had each experienced a kind of meteoric rise in the medical profession. Despite our successes, I suppose we both got bored and developed interests in doing other things. It wasn't long before Couillard and I started meeting for lunch a couple of times a week. I remember having dinner once at his apartment, which was located above a shop in downtown Quebec City. He served fish that night, a fish that he had caught himself, I recall, and we prepared it together with his wife on hand. I even slept over that night.

Fishing became a common theme in our friendship. I had a moderate interest in the sport, but Couillard was passionate. Then again, he was like that with most things he did. Once he had an idea, or decided that he liked something, he pursued it 100 percent. He loved to become an expert at things. He was like that with fishing: he bought the book, the rod and the tackle box, and he and I went on several fishing trips together during my years in Montreal.

When you become a cabinet minister or premier of Quebec, you're expected to have a driver. So off Couillard and I would go, in the back of a government vehicle, usually a minivan driven by a security staffer, the trunk stuffed with fishing equipment and suitcases. Once, we went to New Brunswick for salmon fishing. Another time, he and I travelled via helicopter to Anticosti Island in Quebec, a rather exclusive salmon fishing retreat in the Gulf of Saint Lawrence. Couillard and I would share a log cabin on these trips, rising at 5 AM to push our boat out onto the glassy lake. We would fish until 11 AM, return to the cabin for a big lunch, fish again in the afternoon, and then have a big dinner. We got pleasantly drunk at night, and came to know each other well enough for him to confide in me on a number of matters, and well enough for me to provide support over the years, whether that be financial, professional or psychological. In public positions such as ours, one does not have many friends. It was helpful to have someone I could trust.

Indeed, there was a period when Couillard called me every day, asking what I thought about this issue or that decision. He craved approval, I realized. Couillard wanted to be told that he was doing a good job.

In terms of healthcare policy, Couillard and I rarely butted heads. We each evolved our policies to find a common ground, and if a decision was controversial, he tended to seek my approval first. To be honest, I think he was worried about how I might react to bad news. I was somewhat of a free spirit. Perhaps I might have suggested to him that the emperor was wearing only a loincloth. And Couillard would have done anything to protect his reputation. He would call me to explain that he had to appease the French hospital by being silent and "understanding" when he gave them more money, or by making policy changes that were unfavourable to McGill. "It is only politics," he would say. "I have to do it. You understand. Do not worry. I support the English hospital. It will all get sorted out in the end." It was soon clear to me how badly he wanted to be premier of Quebec. He almost wanted it too badly, in fact.

But despite his faults, I thought he was a very smart man and would make a good premier. He understood Quebec and Canada, and he had a good grasp of international issues too. He was cosmopolitan. And he was a creative and flexible thinker, qualities that I think are key to leadership. Having firm ideas about how to do things is important, but you also need the flexibility of mind to really listen and respond. He had those qualities. When it came to McGill's mega-hospital, however, Couillard struggled like everyone else.

From the beginning, Jean Charest had also assured me that he was on board. I believed him. But the premier was a pragmatist as well. Nobody wanted to stick his or her neck out, Charest least of all. He was gazing into the tea leaves, as if decades of division would suddenly shift, while licking his finger and trying to feel where the winds were blowing.

MONTREAL BADLY NEEDED the mega-hospital. The McGill University Health Centre, formed in 1997, represented the merger of five hospitals: the Montreal General, the Royal Victoria, the Montreal Children's Hospital, the Montreal Neurological Institute and the Montreal Chest Institute. Lachine Hospital would join in 2008. Overall, it was a network with nearly 1,400 beds and more than 14,000 employees serving close to a million patients each year.

While the network was relatively new, the hospitals definitely were not. The Royal Victoria, for example, had been built in 1893. Many areas of the hospital did not have air conditioning, sometimes four beds occupied a single room and superbug infestations were sickening patients at alarming rates.

Superbugs are formed from hospital contaminants in rooms that cannot be adequately cleaned. They live in the walls or in crevices. They can cause terrible bowel illness, bringing on diarrhea and other serious intestinal problems.

At the time I arrived in Montreal, there were several documented deaths at the McGill University Health Centre due to these superbugs. Most patients also became carriers.

The majority of us have sufficient resistance to fight off this kind of infection, but superbugs have a great impact on the weak, the young and the elderly. They are also very hard to treat because, having evolved in a hospital, they become antibiotic-resistant. For these reasons a key feature of the new $1.3-billion mega-hospital was single-patient rooms. In Detroit, we had all but defeated the superbug problem through single-patient room policies. The new hospital rooms in Montreal would also have no sharp edges, making them easier to clean; the floor and wall would blend into a curve to eliminate crevices. I was frequently criticized on both these grounds, though neither plan was terribly unusual. Every suggestion and step forward was met with some kind of delay or opposition.

My critics branded the new mega-hospital "Porter's Hotel," saying I was more concerned with amenities than with the medical side. My true priority, of course, was quite the opposite. In this modern age, you could not start off by designing a hospital for the year 2000. We needed a hospital that reflected its proposed opening date of 2015.

While superbugs were an invisible problem and perhaps harder for people to understand, at least at that time, the sheer dilapidation of the McGill University Health Centre was a less contentious issue. It was more than rooms and hallways appearing worn and in desperate need of paint. The Royal Victoria, for example, sat on the side of a mountain, and had rampant leaks the equivalent of four Olympic-sized swimming pools running through the basement and walls every year. Because the hospital was so old and its architectural plans not well defined, these leaks were almost impossible to fix. We had pumps running constantly. The leaks were especially bad in the winter and when it rained. Over time, many walls simply melted away from moisture. We built new ones and continued with repairs, but only so much could be done. I can say without exaggeration that we spent tens of millions of dollars every year on repairs during my time at the centre.

The state of the hospital was a liability from the patient's point of view, not to mention a gross misappropriation of taxpayers' money. The cost of keeping these buildings going was higher than the value of the hospitals. Every year it was a battle to secure the necessary funds for maintenance. In Detroit, much of our ongoing capital had been spent on repairs. I had one-quarter of the Detroit budget to work with in Montreal. Every year, regardless of expenditure, the hospitals were deteriorating. Renovations would not cut it anymore. The hospital network needed a fresh start.

In addition, I pointed out constantly that the longer we delayed, the more expensive the mega-hospital would be, due to inflation and the price of materials. When I first arrived, the project could have been completed for $800 million. The price tag ended up being $500 million higher than that by the time we broke ground.

From day one in my new position, I put in place an aggressive internal structure to get the job done. What did we want as an institution? What were we trying to achieve? These matters had been discussed endlessly prior to my arrival in Montreal. Under the new regime, once we decided on something and knew what it would look like, the discussion was closed. We then moved on to the next item. Part of the problem was that, in Canada, I was mostly dealing with civil servants who had no "private" money at stake. All they had to do was move paper around their desks and make sure none of it fell off.

THERE WAS NO particular tipping point at which the project finally got underway. The process was simply six long years of skirmishes; constant little fights with executives and various levels of government. It was an exhausting and drawn-out affair, in which each side kept score and fired back at the other at the appropriate time. However, the battle had an entirely different feel from the one in Detroit. Montreal felt more like guerrilla warfare than a stand-up fist fight. It was hard to know who your enemy was. When I saw provincial government officials or influential members of the business community, it was always smiles and handshakes. But when push came to shove, nothing happened the way you expected. Behind closed doors, the same people frowned. Their goal was to delay and make us wait. My goal was to get things done, and sometimes to embarrass.

To drive home the financial reality, I told the press that for every day we delayed, the hospital would cost $100,000 more to build. I even threatened to put up a sign on the mega-hospital's proposed site, similar to those you see in front of McDonalds that read "more than 100 million customers served." My sign would show the perpetual increase in cost. The suggestion did not earn me too many friends, but I made my point.

As we got closer to construction, the various planning authorities often challenged me. Their sole purpose, it seemed, was to block, hamper and delay. The forty-two-acre site for the mega-hospital was the site of the former Glen railyard. Part of the area had also been a dump. It was a huge area, relatively virgin open land in the middle of a small neighbourhood. Decontamination was a constant point of contention and one source of delays. Given my past experiences, I decided to bypass the application for excavation, since I knew it would be denied. I brought in a legion of bulldozers and got started. The bureaucrats did not stop us, though they were more than a little annoyed. I pleaded ignorance. Sorry, I'm new to Quebec, I said. I did not know that we needed to apply for permits before bulldozing. Some might have considered these practices aggressive or unscrupulous. I considered them proactive and progressive. I was tired of the roadblocks. Every time we moved forward, something new would be thrown up in our path to prevent construction. In my mind, *that* was unscrupulous.

Even after McGill's years of planning, every so often the Quebec government would try to reopen the debate on whether we should combine services with the French hospital. As one example, the premier suggested that McGill University Health Centre should offer joint clinical services spread across the city. Anyone in the medical field knew that would be unworkable. Can you imagine telling specialized physicians they had to provide the same service at multiple hospitals throughout Montreal? I had never even heard of the concept, though its proponents managed to give it a name—clinical complementarity. It was a ridiculous and impractical notion. After we shot it down, the government came back and suggested we share laundry and other services. The exercise had descended into farce.

As the years passed by, anxiety also grew that the McGill project had pulled too far ahead of the French hospital. The University of Montreal was finally starting to get its act together, aided by certain key figures in the provincial government. They put the right staffing in place. They even brought in a deputy minister as an advisor. They exhibited a renewed sense of urgency and focus. But it was all too little, too late. By then, my team and I had boxed the province into a series of irrevocable decisions. These were subsequently cemented by the creation of an intricate bidding process for the McGill mega-hospital's construction.

It was agreed that responsibility for the project would be placed in the hands of a public-private partnership, or PPP, a complex process involving the hospital, two government ministries and scores of other people—nearly one hundred participants in total.

In essence, a PPP is a process in which the contracting party determines what it wants to build and then puts a series of specifications out to bid. The successful bidder designs the project, builds it, provides financing and maintains the completed project for a predefined period of time, at the conclusion of which the contracting party can buy the project for a nominal amount.

In a way, the process is like buying a home in a new development. You tell the builder your needs, such as three bedrooms, two bathrooms and a garage, he provides a couple of designs for you to look at, and you choose one of them. The developer then gets you a mortgage and builds the home, and you move in when it's finished.

We set to work on determining what we wanted in the mega-hospital, including the number of rooms for patients, the number and type of operating theatres, labs, kitchens and so on. Teams of experts worked on these specifications. They visited hospitals in Europe and across the U.S., looking for best-in-class and what I would term "future-ready" designs. While this process was going on, a second group was charged with determining who had the skills to do all that was required to build a PPP of this size and complexity, the likes of which had hitherto not been seen in Canada.

So who were these groups of decision makers? Three entities were involved.

The first was Public-Private Partnership Quebec, later known as Infrastructure Quebec, which was an arm of the provincial Ministry of Finance. The second was the Quebec Ministry of Health, through the office responsible for healthcare projects, led by Clermont Gignac, a former project manager for Bombardier. The third group was the McGill University Health Centre. The PPP's ultimate task was to award a 34.25-year contract to design, build, finance and maintain Montreal's new mega-hospital. The group would pay rent, and at the end of the contract, the government would have the ability to purchase the deed for $1. A whole series of rules were established so that the process would be fair. An auditor sat in on every meeting. This was a tried-and-true model that had been successfully administered dozens of times throughout Canada.

Our first step was to decide on the candidates for the bid and qualify them financially. Two consortiums expressed interest and made the cut. One was led by SNC-Lavalin, the largest construction and engineering company in Canada, and by Innisfree Limited, the British infrastructure investment group; the other included companies based in Spain and France.

THE BIDDING PROCESS kicked off with ten separate groups, comprising individuals selected by the two government ministries and the hospital and other analysts, grading these two consortiums based on their pitches. The criteria were quite broad, including everything from patient flow, architectural design and aesthetics to proven experience with heating and cooling large buildings. The consortium led by Innisfree and SNC-Lavalin would eventually achieve the higher score.

But the bidding process involved more than that. There was also the matter of money. Only the provincial government branches had access to the financial details that the two consortiums submitted for the design, construction and execution of the project.

The process appeared to be going well. However, I soon discovered from government authorities that both consortiums were way over our projected budget in their estimates, and not by a few dollars and cents. Both bids were hundreds of millions over the budget we'd set. That was scary. It had taken us years to reach this point. I honestly did not care which consortium won the bid. But I had invested a huge amount of time to reach this stage, and I was concerned that, because the estimates were too high, the Quebec government would disqualify both bidders and retreat to the drawing board. That would have been a disaster.

The naysayers were looking for an excuse to derail the entire process, and, as I had feared, the inflated bids reignited the same objections we had heard from the very beginning. Perhaps we should just renovate the existing McGill hospitals rather than overspend on the bid? Maybe the University of Montreal project should combine with McGill?

The process was saved by a second round of bidding for which the government modified the process and the rules. They asked the McGill hospital group to work with both bidders to modify their wish lists and come up with new plans. These would then be translated by the two bidding consortiums into "best and final offers," or BAFO, that would be reviewed by a new series of committees in an abbreviated fashion. The final decision would be made by a triumvirate: Normand Bergeron, CEO of Infrastructure Quebec; Clermont Gignac, in charge of the modernization of Quebec hospitals; and Arthur Porter, the embattled director general and CEO of McGill University Health Centre.

With Bergeron as our chairman, our job was simply to take all the scoring from the initial review groups and add it up, while making sure everyone was following the rules. The three of us were sealed off in a room, everyone had to sign in and out, and the auditor and Quebec's ethics commissioner were there to ensure it was all done properly. In the end, a fifth-grade student could have polished off the process. The scores spoke for themselves.

Once again, the consortium led by Innisfree and SNC-Lavalin came out on top. Our triumvirate endorsed the decision unanimously to award that consortium the contract to build Montreal's new mega-hospital.

I still think that the PPP made the right decision. SNC-Lavalin was a dynamic, progressive and uniquely global Canadian company, and its consortium stood out in a number of ways. First and foremost was the proposed design, which was gorgeous, clean and curvaceous. We knew Quebecers wanted a hospital that was sleek, modern and a symbol of the future of healthcare in the province.

The French and Spanish consortium's design was bland, square and ugly. It was a utilitarian approach, but what we were seeking was something future-ready, and there was general agreement on that point. Other faults with the competing bid had less to do with its aesthetics. Many committee members were concerned about the overall solidity of the rival consortium. During the process, some of its contractors and subcontractors had dropped out, only to be replaced by others with less experience. The SNC-Lavalin-led consortium had a more consistent base and the right kind of experience.

These were not just my own opinions; the dozens of committee members involved in the bidding process shared them. The auditor who had sat in on the bidding process, André Dumais, would declare in his final report that the process was fair. "On the basis of my observations and verifications, I can confirm that the two bidders have always been treated according to the principles of equality, impartiality and transparency," Dumais wrote.

THE $1.3-BILLION mega-hospital was contentious. There could be no dispute on that point. And those feelings of resentment and bitterness did not simply melt away once the bidding process was completed. If anything, they intensified.

Plenty of people did not want us to succeed. And they especially had not wanted the SNC-Lavalin-led conglomerate to win the bid. SNC-Lavalin was the largest engineering and construction company in Canada, posting global revenues of more than $7 billion. It was one of the most powerful companies in Canada and routinely made substantial donations to political parties, particularly in Quebec. The moment that contract was signed and a PPP came into effect, the conglomerate would run the show. Quebec would not be able to slow down the process. The other bidder, a foreign entity and a relative alien in the province, would have been much easier for the government to stop by finding technicalities and loopholes and generally impeding their progress.

Of course, that did not stop the province from trying to do the same thing with SNC-Lavalin. Shortly after construction began, I received a note saying the site had to be shut down immediately. The hundreds of workers were to stop work because the construction company had erected personnel cabins that were somehow illegal. I cannot recall the actual technicality, but somehow it did not meet code. An injunction was filed, and the bureaucrats gazed at me gleefully, thinking they had finally got us. I told them it was no longer my problem. I sent the injunction by courier to the head office of SNC-Lavalin, giving the top executives a call in advance, just to make sure they knew it was coming. Control over construction was in the consortium's hands now. They had a signed agreement. The issue had nothing to do with McGill University Health Centre. Suffice it to say, crews got back to work in an hour or so. All it took, presumably, was a few phone calls here and there.

The government's impotence to stop what was happening only added fuel to the fire. And SNC-Lavalin would soon become vulnerable, revealing cracks in its once-mighty armour. For many years, the company had been admired for its success overseas. It did business in places few companies had managed to penetrate. Sadly, in the lead-up to the hospital contract, there had been controversies and scandals involving the company in places such as India, Bolivia and most notably Libya. SNC-Lavalin would be targeted for what many considered questionable business practices.

I highlight SNC-Lavalin because the company remained such an intense area of focus for Quebec media and investigators in connection with the mega-hospital. But people forget that it was not SNC-Lavalin that won the bid. It was the consortium of which the company was a part. SNC-Lavalin became a lightning rod, given its association with the province of Quebec. It was by no means the only major player at the table. But the scandals surrounding the company in other places provided more than enough motivation for the hospital project's enemies to pounce.

And then there was Arthur Porter, the CEO and director general at the McGill University Health Centre, seen by some as the catalyst behind this black mark on the province's French establishment. I knew very well that plenty of people were out to get me. In the lead-up to the groundbreaking of the hospital, a friend told me: "They are blaming you for everything in Montreal, including the snow." During and after my tenure in Montreal, I would be targeted for just about everything, although admittedly the $22.5-million fraud charges against me would top the list as the most preposterous. But more on that later; I am getting ahead of myself.

As I said, I did not come to Montreal to be loved. But it was clear to me that, at least in some circles, there was an intense feeling that I could not be controlled. It was bad enough I did not speak French and had never really lived in Quebec. I was not one of them. How many CEOs in the country held a diplomatic passport for an African country? How many were mining and building infrastructure in Sierra Leone and Libya? How many had also been the CEO of a major hospital network in the U.S. and become a known Republican and a friend of George W. Bush?

In truth, I was already planning my resignation once the project was approved.

THE DATE FOR the mega-hospital's groundbreaking was set for April 1, 2010—April Fool's Day, no less. It had been six years to the day, in fact, since I had accepted the post as CEO and director general of the McGill University Health Centre. The giant medical facility would be the largest in Canada, stretching across forty-three acres and integrating five major hospitals, a state-of-the-art research centre and a dedicated oncology department. Separate but closely related was the new Shriners Children's Hospital. For me, six years of dedicated work boiled down to this day.

The day was not exactly going according to plan.

Politicians, businessmen and the mayor sprang from their cars and rushed through a gauntlet. Dozens of Montreal police were in full riot gear, holding back an equal number of protestors waving signs and hurling insults.

Having come from Kenya, Sierra Leone and Detroit, I considered it a rather tame protest—no guns, no tanks, no bodies lying in the streets. I could see, however, that many of the esteemed guests were rattled. I was not going to let a few protestors ruin this moment. Instead of being held on the actual grounds, the event shifted at the last minute to a small community theatre. We tried to maintain calm and order as we guided people into a reception area on the second floor. We could not hear the chants and screams from up there. I circulated through the crowd, smiling, socializing and trying to put guests at ease. But as I scanned the room for those present, I was acutely aware of one who was not: Jean Charest, the premier of Quebec.

Earlier that day, I had arrived in the office to a message waiting for me from Charest's public relations team: the premier would not be making today's event. Word had spread that remnants of the Front de libération du Québec, otherwise known as the FLQ, were planning on crashing the party. The organization, made up of French separatists, rose to notoriety in the 1960s and was responsible for a number of terrorist attacks. In 1969, the FLQ bombed the Montreal Stock Exchange, and just one year later, it murdered a local politician and kidnapped the British trade commissioner. The party mostly fell off the radar over the coming decades, although it tended to rear its head whenever it identified an affront to French rights and sovereignty.

FLQ or no, Charest's absence was unacceptable. After getting the message from his office that morning, I dropped everything and drove straight to see him. There was no sense calling. I arrived at his office at 9 AM and demanded to see him immediately. All I got was his chief of staff, because apparently Charest was unavailable. I told the chief of staff that the premier was making a big mistake. The groundbreaking was going forward whether he arrived or not, and I would say he had "chickened out" because of the protestors.

I did not care about backlash. If there was no groundbreaking, I would be history. If I postponed the event, more delays could be manufactured. Before you knew it, weeks would turn into months. Priorities would change, and suddenly you would no longer be the issue of the day.

We were moving forward with or without him. The course was set. And in many respects, his presence or absence would not have mattered. The contracts had been signed. The ink was dry, and yet denial remained. A few days before the event, I recall that a very senior Quebec politician, Raymond Bachand, called to congratulate me on a job well done. He assured me, however, that the English mega-hospital could never be built before the French one. All of my efforts would be for naught.

And yet there we were, just minutes before the ground-breaking, albeit without a premier. Collective nervousness and anticipation grew as the minutes ticked by. The guests kept looking at their watches. Rumour had it that Charest was on his way, although nobody knew for sure.

At the eleventh hour, only a few minutes before the festivities got underway, Charest arrived. The premier did not brave the gauntlet like the rest of the guests. He slipped in through the back door with his entourage. I had a feeling he would be upset with me after my ultimatum that morning.

None of that mattered once he arrived. It was politics. We smiled and shook hands. I led Charest, the board of directors and everyone else downstairs. The theatre had around a hundred seats, and we took the stage in turn, like a troupe of actors delivering tongue-in-cheek soliloquies. Everyone said the right things. I received a standing ovation. It was announced that one of the streets on the new mega-hospital campus would be named in my honour. We posed for photographs, smiling and laughing in a hail of clicks and flashes. The irony of it all was not lost on me. It was theatre.

Before the curtain fell on this performance, there would be one more act. While we were on stage, the staff had prepared an upstairs room for the final scene. We entered to find a huge cake in the shape of a shovel. On the floor lay some real shovels and a pile of dirt. Charest and I, along with a few others, each took up a shovel and gathered around. But these theatrical flourishes could not disguise the truth.

During my tenure, the McGill University Health Centre had received a $250-million grant for our research institute. Internationally, we had been recognized as one of the province's finest institutions. At home, we had been rec-ognized by the *Globe and Mail* as one of Canada's top one hundred employers, and as one of Montreal's top fifteen employers by the *Montreal Gazette* for several consecutive years.

Building that hospital was probably the hardest deal I had ever closed. Of anything I had done in my life, it had taken the most personal energy. It wasn't easy, and indeed, my challenges were just beginning. But I came, I saw, and I got the job done.

I stuck my shovel in the dirt and took a bow.

top I spent the first years of my life in Boston, USA, while my father completed his PhD. My family soon moved back to my native Sierra Leone. (1957)

above With a Danish mother and African father, my sister and I identified as neither black nor white. That philosophy was not always shared among others during my time spent in Nairobi, Kenya, shortly after the Mau Mau Rebellion. From left: Myself, my cousin Hannah Jones, her mother, Rigmor Jones, my grandmother Emma Malling Rasmussen, my father, Arthur Porter III, and my sister, Emma Adina. (1975)

above left From 1975 to 1984, I earned a bachelor of arts in anatomy, a master's in natural science and a medical degree at Cambridge University. I also served as president of the Cambridge African Union.

above right I prided myself on being a Freemason to the thirty-second degree. Freemasonry ran deep in my family. My father escorted me to Masonic Lodge meetings in Sierra Leone. (1980)

above left My mother and I would often take walks near Sussex Beach in Sierra Leone. My family ate dinner or lunch on the beach when visiting our holiday home. (1980)

above right My wife, Pamela Mattock Porter, would sometimes attend medical conferences with me, such as this trip to Kyoto, Japan. Early in my career, I believed the path to success was visibility, indispensability and working harder than anyone else. (1987)

facing top From left: Gemma Porter, Charlotte Porter, Fiona Porter, Adina Porter and myself during a family vacation in Tennessee. I received my MBA at the University of Tennessee. (1989)

facing bottom With long work schedules and family spread out across the globe, time spent with my family was precious. From left: Adina Porter, Charlotte Porter, myself, Fiona Porter and Gemma Porter Livingston.

above My wife and I first met during our studies at Cambridge University and we never left each other's side for more than three decades. With Pamela as the dependable cornerstone, I was free to pursue lofty ambitions.

above I met with Turkish President Suleyman Demirel, centre, in Ankara during one of my many international medical missions. Noted urologist Edson Pontes, right of Demirel, accompanied me on this occasion. (1997)

facing top Former president of the United States Bill Clinton crossed paths with me in Detroit prior to the election of George W. Bush. I credited Clinton as being the "master" of working a room. (2000)

facing bottom Jennifer Granholm, right, the former governor of Michigan, proved to be a worthy opponent during my tumultuous days at the helm of the Detroit Medical Centre.

top From left: former U.S. president George Bush, his wife, Laura Bush, and myself. After I had turned down an appointment as Surgeon General of the United States, Bush called me at home to see if I would reconsider. I once again declined.

above From left: former vice president of the United States Dick Cheney, myself, and U.S. Representative for Michigan and Chairman of the Permanent Select Committee on Intelligence, Mike Rogers. I considered myself a fiscal Republican, but with social views leaning closer to those of the Democrats.

top Michaëlle Jean, the former Governor General of Canada, presided over my induction to the Queen's Privy Council for Canada. (2008)

above From left: Myself, Prime Minister Stephen Harper and former senator David Angus. Throughout my time in Canada, I would remain a staunch Conservative. I strongly believed you could change the country in which you lived, but should never change your political stripes.

top I always enjoyed a drink and a long chat with my father, Arthur Porter III, seen here in Nassau, Bahamas. My father, a noted historian in Sierra Leone, instilled in me a lasting sense of African pride and nationalism. (2011)

above From the construction of the Cancer Centre in in 2002, the Bahamas played an important role in my business and professional life. Nassau soon became home base for my family and me. From left: Adina Porter, myself and Fiona Porter enjoy a weekend away in Harbour Island, Eleuthera. (2012)

top Ernest Bai Koroma, left, the president of Sierra Leone, remained a close friend throughout my life. With David Allen, president of Africa Infrastructure Group, far side, and Vincent Kanu, a board member, we discussed business proposals in the president's office.

above During my initial battle with cancer, I decided to shave my head completely. With a "chemotherapy-induced haircut," I wore traditional dress while posing with the Sierra Leonean flag. Although my country of birth had its political troubles, I was always proud of my African heritage. (2013)

above My eldest daughter got married in the Bahamas a few months after my cancer diagnosis. The service was attended by a small gathering of close friends and family. From left: Fiona Porter, Adina Porter, myself, Ryan Livingston, Gemma Porter Livingston, Pamela Mattock Porter and Charlotte Porter. (2013)

8.

NOTHING
IS PRIVATE
ANYMORE

***

IN THE SUMMER of 2008, David Penner, the director of appointments in Ottawa, asked if I would come down to Ottawa for a meeting.

The process of naming high-level appointments in Canada was similar to the American one. Up to three hundred positions needed to be filled. The government kept a list of potential candidates, people who could be useful in a number of ways. I was a known Conservative by then, having built a reputation for myself in Montreal. I had close relationships with leaders in the party. I routinely attended party fundraisers and events. Meanwhile, I was a doctor, born in Africa and with a strong background in internationalism. It ticked all of the right boxes. Two years earlier, in fact, I had been appointed in just this way to the governing council of the Canadian Institutes of Health Research in Canada, a body that oversaw government funding for health-related research. I had not been surprised to get that call. After all, I was a researcher by reputation and already running one of the largest hospital networks in the country.

But this latest call, I can tell you, was something of a surprise. Penner did not say what the meeting was about, other than simply to talk about my life and career trajectory, but I had my suspicions. Rumours had reached me that a spot was opening on the board for the Security Intelligence Review Committee. In the hierarchy of intriguing appointments, it trumped the research gig.

So, in the lead-up to my meeting in Ottawa, I did my homework. And the more I learned, the more I saw that I was rather well suited for the role. I knew what those new job title initials would stand for, and I came to the table armed with ideas.

When Penner and I met, I made it clear that I was interested. And it was obvious the government was interested in me, because weeks later, after the board member retired, I got a call inviting me to the screening process. I agreed without hesitation. After all, I had already experienced a full-field investigation in the U.S. during my campaign for surgeon general. And as it turned out, the Canadian screening process was far less rigorous. I did not have extended conversations with members of CSIS. Nobody came to my home. Whether extensive investigations occurred in the background, I do not know. I certainly never heard of it, so I suppose that, if they did look into me, they were satisfied. My appointment was put forth by both the prime minister and the governor general, although as a courtesy, Harper sent a letter to the other parties. The Liberals were fine with it. The New Democratic Party approved. The only party that gave me thumbs-down was the Bloc Québécois. That came as little surprise. I was too right-wing, the party said, too Republican and close to George W Bush. The party also alluded to perceived mismanagement back at the Detroit Medical Center.

The real issue, of course, was my position within the English establishment in Quebec. I was also not a Quebecer, and in the end I was taking a seat they would prefer to be French. In truth, a member of the Conservatives later told me that the Bloc Québécois had a tendency to reject candidates. The prime minister actually saw their refusal as a political bonus. He was not seeking real approval anyway.

So in September 2008, at a ceremony in Ottawa, I swore allegiance to Canada and the Queen and accepted my elevated position as privy councillor. I was now the Honourable Arthur Porter. I received a huge certificate and heightened security clearance. When I die, the flag flying above Parliament will be brought to half-mast.

WITHIN A YEAR of this appointment, the prime minister would again call upon me.

The United Nations Security Council, established in 1946, was charged with peacekeeping operations, international sanctions and authorization of military action. Only five nations hold permanent, veto-wielding membership: China, the U.S., Russia, France and the U.K. Add ten nonpermanent members, with five elected each year, for a total of fifteen. Canada had always been a fixture on council, achieving a coveted elected spot every time we campaigned.

Under normal circumstances, Canada would enter into an election year full of confidence. But things had changed. I got a call from Harper in 2009. The Conservatives realized that they were going to lose the election in 2010, and really they had done no lobbying or campaigning to earn a victory.

Since the Tories had taken power, there was an acute sense that the developing world did not favour Canada in the upcoming vote. As I was a known Conservative, originally from Sierra Leone and with access to heads of state in Africa and the Caribbean, Harper tasked me with speaking to as many leaders as possible. He wanted to find out what it would take to win that seat.

I travelled to a number of countries in the months leading up to the election, including my native Sierra Leone, Nigeria, Ghana, Jamaica, Antigua and Barbuda, and Trinidad and Tobago. I fielded many phone calls and met with representatives from various countries at the United Nations in New York City. As I engaged in discussions, it quickly became clear that perceptions of Canada had changed. In years past, Canada had always been very liberal, particularly in sending aid to Africa. The Harper administration had placed more restrictions on funding, and aid was often administered through international organizations such as the World Bank or the International Monetary Fund, rather than more directly.

Every prime minister has his or her strengths. From an economic perspective, Harper was outstanding. Where he faltered was in the international arena. He came from Alberta and, particularly in the beginning, surrounded himself with hometown loyalists, none of whom proved effective in international relations. So, in 2009, Harper was often pegged as an isolationist. I do not know whether he had travelled much before becoming prime minister. I am nearly certain he had never been to Africa. Combined with his more reserved personality, I could understand why the developing world did not find him approachable.

My job was damage control, to explain to leaders and

representatives with whom I met that, while the government had changed, Canada's international values had not.
We were prepared to develop different strategies in order to
facilitate more cordial international relationships.

As it turned out, my efforts proved to be too little, too
late. Portugal and Germany won that campaign. It was
clear we could have got a seat if we had played our cards
right. Much was made of Canada's strong support of Israel
and losing favour among the Arabs states. Certainly, that
factor was at play, but lost ground in the developing world
at large was our downfall—a place where Canada, in the
past, had enjoyed exemplary status.

I found it noteworthy that many leaders thought of
Harper as a mini-Bush. Our policies and agendas were perceived as too closely aligned with those of the U.S. Whether
these observations were accurate or not is debatable, and
largely irrelevant. What was at stake, in my view, was the
loss of our historical identity abroad. Harper decided that
he could not be everything to everyone. He wanted to be
known among the Group of Eight, the superpowers of the
world, as opposed to the G138 club.

That seat at the big-boy table is important, but so is our
stature elsewhere. It was that reputation that made Canada
a unique place in the world, commanding a unique type of
respect. If our failure with the UN Security Council taught
us anything, it was Canada's risk of becoming somewhat
of a mini-America, rather than a moderate, friendly, mid-
dle-of-the-road nation. Although the government abandoned its 2014 bid for a seat on the Council, I still believe
that Canada could and should try again. We must start
much earlier, open up and become more consistent in our
messaging.

MY WORK FOR Harper concerning the United Nations Security Council was important. But I considered it a side job. My first priority was the Security Intelligence Review Committee, and in particular sniffing out the pecking order. The watchdog of the Canadian secret service had five people on the board, including the chairman. The rest of the office comprised thirty or so employees, mostly made up of intelligence analysts and lawyers, as one of our duties was to conduct legal hearings of cases that had national security implications.

First and foremost, the Security Intelligence Review Committee provides "near time" review of the secret service and other issues of national security. Its process differs considerably from that of the U.S. Our counterpart, the Senate Select Committee on Intelligence, has outright oversight of the CIA. It has an ongoing dialogue and can shape actions before they happen. In Canada, we review decisions and operations shortly after the fact, and subsequently provide recommendations on future policy or further actions.

Our review of the secret service involved formal requests whereby we would ask a series of questions or seek documents on a particular subject and within a designated time frame. The key was making the requests precise enough that CSIS would be forced to provide some kind of information. So every year I would choose six topics I was interested in. We would ask the questions, CSIS would duck and dodge and pretend they did not have everything we asked for, and we would often send investigators to follow up—but always with the blessing of CSIS. Our board would review the information and decide what was sensitive or confidential, and then write a report for the minister of public security. That was the official process, and CSIS would comply with our recommendations nine out of ten times, if not ten out of ten.

When I was portrayed in the media (often in a negative light), I would typically be described as having "access to Canada's most carefully guarded secrets." I was certainly privy to secrets and issues of national security. However, I did not spend my days poring over classified documents in an underground bunker while pulling the world's strings.

Granted, many of the documents I was responsible for could not leave Ottawa unless someone from the RCMP accompanied them. If I were in Montreal, for example, an armed officer would arrive in my office with a special brief-case. I would read the documents with him standing over me while I made notes. I also had an imploding briefcase for my personal documents, the kind that destroyed all of its contents when you got the combination wrong.

But in truth, 90 percent of what passed over my desk was not of the utmost secrecy. The general public might not know, for instance, that during my tenure there were twenty-two unmarked police cars in Ottawa. But disclosure of this classified information wouldn't cause damage, or even surprise too many people. Is it an important secret? Probably not. However, if there were torture chambers under Rideau Hall—which, I can assure you, there are not—then that would be a rather important secret, with more serious fallout if disclosed.

My point is, only a small percentage of classified information would be considered coveted secrets, the kind we take to our graves.

One of the most common issues we faced was complaints against the secret service by everyday Canadians. A steady stream of people felt harassed, threatened or hurt. For example, if the secret service was investigating a person of interest, someone might complain that agents were harassing him or her at work. A complaint could be filed, and my board became the judiciary at our chambers just behind Queen Street in Ottawa, in the Blackburn Building.

In any given year, around ten cases would go to trial. The government received far more complaints than that, and we divided them into two piles. There were the nutters, so to speak, the kind of people who also had voices talking to them. And then you had the ones with legitimate concerns. Only 30 percent of our complaints could be slotted into the second category. We would examine those situations quite closely.

As I had done my whole life, I took on a leadership position from the beginning. I was a vocal contributor every six weeks, when we had our formal meeting of all members. I did not blend in. And before long, I was working harder than everyone else. I took on more cases of Canadians alleging harassment. And I focused on trying to make the Security Intelligence Review Committee better. I liked the Canadian system of review, provided it was done in real time.

I pushed for greater efficiencies, often in terms of the time it took to address cases. When I arrived, we were taking upwards of a year to review anything. My opinion was, if it takes more than a year to review a case, it becomes increasingly less applicable or relevant to Canadian society. It was no longer timely, not to mention the fact that evidence and testimony become increasingly stale. There was too much red tape. People worked slowly and there were always problems accessing witnesses or data. It was being run like an academic show rather than a process in the pub-lic's interest.

Canadians might have been surprised, even amazed that I was appointed to the Security Intelligence Review Committee and then became chairman in 2010. After all, although I began my medical practice in Canada, I had lived outside the country for many years. My critics pointed to my extensive experience in the U.S. and Sierra Leone, and certainly my run-ins in Detroit didn't always help my reputation. But the reasons for my appointment were actu-ally quite clear, when you think about it.

The Canadian Security Intelligence Service itself was a changing organization. The twenty-first century brought new threats, many of which stemmed from so-called new Canadians, or ethnic minorities, with considerable language and cultural differences. We were dealing with people of interest who typically did not have the name John Smith.

As the face of the enemy changed, the secret service had to keep pace and change its makeup so it wasn't just one white guy from Alberta, another from Saskatchewan and so on. Canada needed a truly global service that thought dif-ferently and recognized what the new Canada looked like.

During the Cold War, Canada's enemies were far more obvious. It was easy to conceptualize and target a specific threat somewhere halfway around the world. When I joined SIRC, our focus was often on the enemy in our backyard. We were dealing with young, bored or angry people who by all legal accounts were truly Canadian. Their parents might have been born elsewhere, and perhaps they did not speak English well, but they were just as Canadian as anyone else. Much was always made of the homegrown terrorism issues in the U.S. In Canada, these individuals also represented a very real security risk. They were people to watch. One could argue that Canada's commitment to multiculturalism, and to maintaining a "mosaic" of people, only amplified these risks.

When my children attended school in Michigan, they rose before the flag that stood beside the chalkboard at the front of the classroom and pledged their allegiance to the United States of America. It was a melting pot, with national identity coming first. While Canadian children also rise to sing "O Canada," that country does not have nearly the same degree of nationalism and push to conformity as the U.S. does. Canada prides itself on being a multi-cultural society, one that allows for, and even embraces, separate identities.

While many people might praise this open-mindedness, it also has drawbacks from a security point of view. Canada allows all its citizens not only their own cultures, but also their own gripes. They can fight their wars not only abroad, but also in Canada. Many of the issues Canada faced, in my view, grew from this diluted sense of nationalism and from what was happening in the rest of the world.

It was one of the problems with Canadian identity, or perhaps the lack thereof. In my view, Canadians should be Canadian. The issue of "half-Canadians" and national security will only get worse over time.

The Internet made these threats even greater. With the click of a mouse, young jihadists had a graphic window onto war-torn lands. They could see the destruction in places such as Afghanistan and interact through email and chat rooms. Suddenly, given the right circumstances, that virtual portal could seem more real than their adopted homeland. Alienation deepened.

The Omar Khadr incident was a perfect example. Khadr, a fifteen-year-old Canadian citizen, was captured by American forces following a firefight in Afghanistan. He nearly died from his wounds. Canada was heavily criticized for allowing him to languish in Guantanamo Bay for so many years, the last Western citizen to be held there. Here was a young man, born in Toronto, the son of Egyptian immigrants, who through his father's work spent a great deal of time in Pakistan. Whether through his family or otherwise, his terrorist connections came to rival and indeed overwhelm the North American frame of mind.

Is there such a thing as a true Canadian? Should Canada have demanded better treatment for him from the Americans? Should we have wrenched him from Guantanamo?

I was not yet on the board when Khadr was banished to Gitmo. But I was on the board when the issue became a source of embarrassment for the country. As board member and then chairman, I had to face these difficult questions. They were especially difficult for me because I believe our approach had been wrong. The man got tortured at Gitmo. And in turning him away, we were not banishing him from Quebec to, say, British Columbia. We should have recognized what was going to happen. In hindsight, we acknowledged that there could have been a better way, in terms of bringing him back and reintegrating him into society. We need to spend more time understanding and learning from young men like Omar Khadr, taking a close look at how we educate and socialize new Canadians.

As a review committee, one of the biggest and most fundamental questions we asked ourselves concerned the future of the Canadian secret service. What do we want it to be?

Many people do not realize that the Canadian Secret Intelligence Service is not a foreign spy agency like the CIA in America, Mossad in Israel, MI6 in the U.K. or the FSB (formerly the KGB) in Russia. In the U.S., I can assure you, there are at least a dozen agencies that most people have never heard of. In Canada, we only had CSIS, and generally speaking, they told countries that they were coming.

In other words, our secret service was typically Canadian. Their agents could not take passports from Britain, go to a hotel in France and assassinate a bunch of Arabs. Canada would never put our agents at mortal risk. Nobody wanted Canadians to die, although sometimes they died anyway.

I recall one incident when a country that was not exactly a close friend of Canada captured a handful of our agents who had been acting without the formal approval of the secret service, taking photos of tanks and other military equipment. In this case, the Canadians ended up losing their lives. They were tortured and hanged. We had to keep the truth of how they died from their families, telling them instead that they fell off a balcony in Dubai, for example. None of these incidents ever made the papers, and they were not isolated incidents. For whatever reason, agents sometimes went rogue, a bit too James Bond, and stretched the limits of their official position.

THE IDENTITY AND role of Canada's secret service was the subject of my final report as chairman of the Security Intelligence Review Committee. I was asking the question that we had avoided for decades: Should we maintain what we have, or establish a true foreign intelligence service? The fact was, we were beginning to stray towards the latter. I was not against the creation of a proper foreign service at all, but only if we had the right backup, structure and support. We could not do Mickey Mouse raids and hope it would work out. Many colleagues of mine felt that Canada's place in the world warranted a legitimate foreign service, especially if we wanted a seat at the big-boy table. I believe some colleagues just wanted to have a foreign service because it looked good on their sleeve. They reminisced about their counterparts in other areas of the world and how lucky they were. Other agencies had so much freedom. Meanwhile, the Canadian secret service had to fret about a couple of bullets. Creating a foreign service, however, was no simple task. We had many important questions to answer.

The first was financial. It would take half a billion dollars per year, at minimum, to create that foreign capacity. As it was, we always had to consider how a particular incident or decision would look on the front page of Canadian dailies. How can we justify thirty million Canadians contributing $10 each to keep us in business next year? Money was a big point of discussion already, and I could not see Canada taking the secret service to the next level from an economic point of view.

The second question was more philosophical. It cut to the heart of what it meant to be Canadian. Did we have the stomach for it? Could the Canadian government, and indeed citizens at large, accept having a foreign service that breaks the laws of other countries? Such activities were commonplace among other agencies at the big-boy table. I remember discussing this point with Harper face to face. The problem with Canada is that it is full of Canadians. We are not like the Americans, Russians or Israelis. If our agents are caught and executed, can we handle that? Can we deny knowledge of them?

In my view, Canada was not a big enough country to warrant a true foreign service. We also lacked the financial and philosophical commitment. And we did not have impending threats sufficient to warrant taking such a risk.

Canada's attitude towards torture and interrogation techniques seems to me its own answer to these questions. Our policy was somewhat hands-off; we liked to have other people do the dirty work. In other words, we wrote down the questions and let someone else go into the room. To be honest, I never liked this position either. As in the debate over a foreign service, I disagreed with having a half-in, half-out strategy. Either we were in Afghanistan and fighting a war, or we were not.

War comes with casualties. It also comes with prisoners, and subsequently, what we refer to as "enhanced interrogation techniques." But when push came to shove, Canada preferred to take a back seat. Sometimes we would hand it off to other governments. Other times we would work with local authorities and segments of the police force or military. They were perfectly happy to do these things. And we would pay for the service, but never in cash. It was always in kind. We told ourselves that we had a certain standard of behaviour in Canada. Members of the military, which did the handing off, did not always agree with the policy. Some would argue it was silly to fight a war in another country, such as Afghanistan, and apply the same standards as we would in Mississauga. These soldiers had improvised explosive devices blowing them to bits and snipers targeting them from rooftops in burnt-out villages. Soldiers wanted to fight fire with fire, and to an extent I agreed with them. These were the realities of war in a foreign place. When we decided to go in there, we had to think about these positions and make decisions beforehand, not after we went in. We also knew full well what was being done to the prisoners after they were handed over. Does turning a blind eye make us any less culpable?

Rather than face head-on these ugly realities and contradictions, I instead highlighted what else Canada might bring to the table.

In 2013, Edward Snowden, a systems administrator from North Carolina who leaked details on classified mass surveillance programs in the U.S. and the U.K., captured the world's attention. (I always found it intriguing that the substance of the leaks more or less took a back seat to the drama surrounding Snowden. Any person on the street could probably tell you how he evaded capture in Hong Kong, managed to get on a plane to Russia and spent months holed up in an airport while seeking asylum in South America. The so-called Snowden soap opera was mostly what people cared about. If I asked the same people what the leaks actually were, they probably could not tell me with any real accuracy.)

Leaks happen all the time. The Snowden affair only confirmed what most people already suspected: people are watching us. In Canada, as everywhere else, nothing is private anymore. It has taken the Canadian media a long time to see that. But Snowden's moment in the sun is finite. In truth, the information he leaked is of little consequence. These days, what is far more important is not the information itself, but information analysis. It is how a country has chosen to interpret and act on the facts, as opposed to the facts themselves.

America is not the only country with advanced surveillance techniques. There is a less visible branch of the Canadian secret service completely dedicated to surveillance, which did not fall under my review. Communications Security Establishment Canada was mostly unregulated, with a commissioner at its helm and no board of directors. The commissioner reported only to the minister of national defense. As head of the watchdog of the Canadian Security Intelligence Service, I was only aware of its existence and understood some of its basic operations and processes. It rarely worked with us. That alone should give you an idea of its classified role in the murky world of surveillance.

Communications Security Establishment Canada has been around since the Second World War, although most citizens have probably never heard of it. In the wake of 9/11, the department has been on the rise, with a new $1-billion head office set to open in 2015. While I did not work directly with the department, its personnel are quite good at their jobs, and the department often works in cooperation with its counterparts in the U.S., such as the National Security Agency. There is not a free flow of information. Canada provides it on a request basis. The Americans do the same. It is a bartering of secrets and lives, the sharing of countless private moments. The departments are entirely separate entities. But in a sense, they also constitute an informal North American network of spies.

Surveillance today consists of computers, incredible technological systems continuously monitoring every phone call, text message and email in the country, looking for trends and red flags. Bomb. Al-Qaeda. Bin Laden. The system works off complex algorithms that identify repeated words, or words used in specific sequences, until it gradually filters into a smaller list of potential threats.

Think of it as a road sweep. Imagine if the government started stopping every car on the street for no apparent purpose, just to stick their nose in the driver-side window and pop the trunk. It would never fly. There would be public outrage. Police need cause to stop the car, such as speeding or running a red light. But what if you could search every car without having to stop them?

What these activities lead to is specific tapping and surveillance. The authorization to do this is quite easy to get. It always depends on the circumstances and threat level at the time, but targeted surveillance could easily be done within the hour, or sometimes less. Sometimes, in the interest of expediency, authorization slipped through the cracks.

Technological devices have penetrated our lives to such a degree, and so underpin the transfer of information, that it makes them invaluable tools for surveillance. In the U.S., most devices manufactured in the country must pass through screening by the CIA or some other agency. Smart phones, tablets and laptops can become effective back-door portals to extract information, should the need arise. It is a fast-track system, if you will, allowing analysts to skip the step of casting a wide net and filtering down. Maybe they already know who they are looking for. In Canada, many technologies manufactured in the country are not free from this scrutiny. Canadian telecommunications companies, even those praised for their security, are often privy to these device approvals and specifications. As I said, nothing is private anymore. All information has become fair game.

I believe we live in a Brave New World. While surveillance will continue to spark hot debate, it is a reality we'd better get accustomed to. If Canada is not doing it, someone else will. In fact, they already are, and it is essential we stay ahead of the curve. Canada cannot turn back the clock. We cannot tell students in schools to stop using calculators during a test, even though they were once forbidden. It is not cheating if everyone else does it. Technology shapes the world we live in. Sometimes I wish we did not have the Internet and online surveillance. But we do, and if these tools are available, we need to make the best of them.

In many respects, our aptitude at surveillance has become our bread and butter. We do not have to torture villagers for information or send spies into hostile territory and take photos of nuclear armaments. Canada can find its place in the world, and stay in the know, through the trading of information. It is indeed a highly valued commodity, and prices are rising. Maybe our business is not keeping the world safe. Leave that to the Americans. They appear to enjoy it well enough. What we need to do is keep Canada safe—end of story.

I made this argument to the board and the highest levels of government. The future is surveillance and data analysis, not cloak and dagger. If we want a foreign service, do not think about what it would look like today, but in 2030.

The fact that CSEC is constructing new headquarters, right beside CSIS, is a major step in the right direction. During my tenure, there was talk about physically linking the two buildings. And from what I understand, a physical bridge between the two buildings seems to be in the cards. In this vein, I do see the Canadian secret service melding over the coming years. Departments will change their focus as technology and surveillance take centre stage. Canada should continue to be a national security service, protecting Canadians while also embracing the rising importance of surveillance in lieu of a foreign service.

The billion-dollar question, of course, is how we balance surveillance with our civil liberties. Many people in the know would argue that 9/11 never would have happened if we had used these advanced techniques. The argument is: do not wait until there is such a high level of suspicion to act; nip it in the bud before it becomes an issue of national security. If Canadians have such an issue with surveillance, the most obvious question is: What do they have to hide? Granted, a principle is at stake in terms of our basic freedoms. But again, I would urge these pundits to open their eyes. In our parents' day, there were not so many threats. There were not highly sophisticated organizations looking to hijack planes and fly them into buildings. There were not bombs controlled by cell phone signals. They did not live in a world of such intense globalization, where the face of the enemy is blurred.

The threats have changed, and the world must change with them.

9.

WHEN
IN ROME...

I WAS TUCKING into lunch with my wife and daughters at the Old Fort Bay Club in the Bahamas when my phone vibrated on the white linen. I thought about letting it go. The steaming red snapper, peas, rice, conch salad and plantains set before me—a true Bahamian feast—were far more enticing than another business call. Sitting on the club's patio, surrounded by palm trees, I could hear the waves crashing in the distance.

It was August 2011, and I was having a good day. I was still CEO of the McGill University Health Centre, construction was now underway on the mega-hospital, and I was spending time at my home in the Bahamas, as I did most weekends when I wasn't away on SIRC business. The air was hot yet comfortable, with an ocean breeze, and I tried to ignore that buzzing phone. Nevertheless, I could not resist a peek. It was a 218 area code. I recognized the call's origin, and excused myself from the table.

I walked to the patio's edge, out of earshot, before answering the call.

"Arthur?" a voice echoed, sounding distant. "Arthur, can you hear me?"

"Not well. You are breaking up. Who is this?" I asked.

The person on the other end went quiet for a few seconds. "Hello? Arthur? Is this better? Arthur, it's Riadh." Riadh Ben Aissa was the chief operating officer of SNC-Lavalin.

"Oh, Riadh! How are you, my friend? Yes, I can hear you better now."

"I'm fine, Arthur," he said hastily. I could tell from his voice that this was not a courtesy call. "But look, Pierre and I need a favour." Pierre Duhaime, the CEO, was a charismatic leader and a man I respected highly. "We're in Tripoli right now. Saadi is in the next room and we're talking about this damn war. I need you to speak with him. See if you can convince him to intercede with his father. Will you give it a shot?"

Al-Saadi Gaddafi, the third son of Libyan leader Muammar Gaddafi, was in a tough spot. At this time, he was the commander of Libya's special forces and a key player in the loyalist cause. The North African nation had been in the grips of a brutal civil war for months. In February, two months into the Arab Spring, security forces fired on a group of anti-Gaddafi protestors, providing the spark for a rebellion that exploded throughout the country. Saadi and the loyalist forces had rallied in recent months, taking back several important cities, but by the end of that summer the rebels, with considerable assistance from the international community, had seized the momentum and pushed the Gaddafi regime to the brink.

A subsidiary of SNC-Lavalin, known as SNC-Lavalin International, had been in Libya for more than a decade, building oil refineries and other infrastructure projects. The Libyan partnership had proved to be one of the company's most successful forays in Africa. Top executives at the Canadian multinational were friends with Muammar Gaddafi and his family, and many of SNC-Lavalin's contracts came directly from the top.

The civil war had been bad for business. Prior to the conflict, nobody raised too many eyebrows. Libya was simply just one more arrow, albeit a very important one, in the company's international quiver. It was all business as usual until Libya became a so-called "bad country."

SNC-LAVALIN HAD asked me to work for this division in 2005, shortly after my arrival in Montreal. In fact, it had been the first of several companies to approach me for help with their international expansions. My links and business interests in Africa were well known, and I was considered useful as a consultant.

I was very interested. I knew that Montreal would be my last stint as a hospital administrator. The day-to-day running of the mega-hospital was going to be much less exciting than getting it built, and I had quickly begun to cultivate the next phase of my career in international business. And I liked Pierre Duhaime very much. He was a funny, flashy and aggressive executive. He was small in stature but huge in influence and business acumen. He came out of the mining side of SNC-Lavalin and knew how to deal with people. He was forward-thinking and focused on making things happen. In that respect, he and I got along quite well. I had similar drive and ambition.

Believing that I would be in high demand, SNC-Lavalin was interested in getting a contractual relationship going. I told them that they would have to wait until the hospital got underway before I would sign on with them. After all, they were part of a consortium bidding for the $1.3-billion contract to build and operate the facility.

We drafted legal documents on the terms of my consultancy, effective once the bidding process had ended. In the meantime, I offered to do some informal, unpaid work on their behalf. I wrote a few letters to friends in Africa and put people in touch. If I saw strong leads, I passed them on—nothing more.

Once that shovel pierced earth at the groundbreaking on April 1, 2010, however, I was free and clear to pursue other interests.

That knowledge came as a huge relief. When I first took the job in Montreal, my plan had been to serve one four-year term. I was forced to stay on longer because it took so much time, energy and cajoling to get the mega-hospital built. After the groundbreaking, I tendered my resignation once again. I was not interested in the day-to-day job of being a hospital administrator. I had been there. I already had the hard hat.

However, there was no clear succession plan in place for my position, nobody to step in and take the helm. I was considered something of a hero at the time. I had finally succeeded in getting the mega-hospital started, a feat nobody else could achieve. They would be sheep without a shepherd. That they urged me to stay is well documented, as are my repeated resignations. I explained to the board of directors that they would see less and less of me if I stayed. The only way I would consider it, I said, was if they allowed me to do what I wished in the international arena. They readily agreed.

In a letter dated September 11, 2010, sent to David Angus, then a senator and chairman of the McGill University Health Centre, I explained:

> As you are also aware, I have always had outside inter-
> ests and activities, which have always been agreed upon
> internally—at the initiation of my first contract, at my
> second mandate and at each time that there was a mate-
> rial change.
>
> However some of these activities have changed, have
> become more politically sensitive or now require more of
> my time. I therefore felt that it was necessary to have a
> full and frank discussion with you as Chair of the Board
> of the MUHC, on my current activities, the thoughts that
> I have on our future relationship and some of the risks
> associated with my outside activities.

Angus and I were very close, and he was a keen supporter of the McGill University Health Centre project. When nec-essary, he stepped in to negotiate some difficult decisions, and he was instrumental in keeping things on track. Mean-while, Angus knew everything I was doing. We spoke every second day, and those conversations involved not only my dealings at the health centre, but also what I was doing in my other businesses. I even sent him a copy of my diplo-matic appointment in Sierra Leone. Angus was a terrific guy. He came from the older Conservative guard and had served as a close ally to former Canadian prime minister Brian Mulroney. Consequently, he was never too close with Ste-phen Harper, who represented the Alberta style of conser-vatism, more humble and focused on hard work and family values.

Angus was the kind of guy one would find in the estab-lished gentlemen's clubs, a cigar in one hand and a stiff drink in the other, with others of his stripe, asking one another if they'd ever met a poor person. I am being face-tious, of course, but Angus clearly came from a more afflu-ent background. His father had been a member of the Royal Montreal Club. I was also a member, and I recall entering the bar with him one day, when the good senator pointed to the ground.

With a certain dry wit, he said: "That is where my father collapsed."

In fact, his father *had* died right there at the bar. I don't know how he died exactly; I did not inquire further. I sus-pect it was a heart attack. But he didn't spill his drink, I was told. It was that sort of place.

That kind of offbeat humour was not unusual for Angus. He once told me: "Arthur, as you get older, remember: never trust a fart, and never waste an erection."

But I digress. I only provide this background to show how close I was with Angus, and how well aware he was of my affairs.

I told Angus and the health centre board, both in the let-ter and face to face, that my deals with outside parties might be public, and sometimes agreements go sour or become part of the public interest. And the board insisted that they were comfortable with the arrangement.

With that approval, I started pursuing a number of proj-ects on behalf of SNC-Lavalin. We looked at constructing a new oil refinery in Sierra Leone, for example, and a whole industrial city in Saudi Arabia. Among other initiatives, I began helping to facilitate their marriage making and brokering.

Many of the deals I knew little about from a practical point of view. I knew nothing about refineries and how they actually functioned, or what they cost. But I knew one country that needed one, and this company wanted to build and finance it. And I was good at bringing people to the table. That has always been my talent throughout my career, whether in medicine, politics or business.

I had the equivalent of ten full-time jobs in 2010. In addition to my activities with SNC-Lavalin, I had other Canadian mining companies doing robust business in Sierra Leone. In Canada, I was chairman of the Special Committee of Canadian Royalties when the Chinese firm Jilin Jien Nickel Industry Company Limited completed its acquisition of the mining company. Meantime, while I was on the board of directors at Air Canada, I had interests in expanding the airlift into West Africa, especially for Sierra Leone. On the medical side, I was the chairman of a Florida-based manufacturer for radiotherapy equipment. Of course, I was also overseeing the Cancer Centre and other businesses in the Bahamas while expanding the clinic's brand throughout the Caribbean.

Around this time, Philippe Couillard took a break from politics, and we decided to go into a healthcare consulting business together, focused mainly in the Middle East, a region that particularly interested him, as he had practised neurological surgery in Saudi Arabia for a couple of years. We had some bites, and I think the business could have really taken off. But the timing was not right. He was finished with being minister of health and eager to get going. I already had a lot going on, and was still completing the McGill University Health Centre. I just did not have time to stick a fork into everything on my plate.

I think people often muddled SNC-Lavalin's strong interest in my international skills with its bid for the hospital contract. It was an unfortunate misperception. Certainly a company of such power and influence did not need an anglophone newcomer to Montreal to pull strings in Quebec; they already had those strings around their fingers. What they needed was someone who could get the job done in Africa.

I often got paid up front for my consulting, or I was given a piece of the business, or perhaps both. I wanted to get paid whether the deal closed or not, and most of the time it did, which was why I could command those terms. SNC-Lavalin had an interesting way of paying. With several projects in countries located in Africa and Asia, it basically overwrote the money it would spend there. So it had these "slush pockets" of cash attached to these projects. I would be paid in one area, but the expectation was that I would consult as the opportunities arose.

In other words, the payment and work were not always geographically aligned.

During this time I was working almost exclusively with SNC-Lavalin's central leadership, including the chairman, the president/CEO and occasionally the chief financial officer. I was not working in international consulting quite as much as I wanted, due to my ongoing duties in Montreal. But I was able to produce interesting leads to some very lucrative deals. People were making money. And I resisted any Canadian links in my dealings. I recall being approached to help with a contract for building Canadian army vehicles. I had no interest in jeopardizing my political position, and instead I found them a consultant and lobbyist to replace me, someone even better connected in the Conservative Party who could meet their needs. Bernard

Lord, a friend and the former premier of New Brunswick, fit the bill perfectly.

It was all going splendidly, until Libya blew it wide open.

Times had changed. SNC-Lavalin had once been one of the most favoured companies in Quebec, if not all of Canada. But its activities in Libya, while nothing new, had cast a dark cloud over everything. SNC-Lavalin was not accustomed to being on the losing side. My call with Gaddafi wasn't the first time SNC-Lavalin had sought my help in Libya. A few months earlier, I had received a call from Pierre Duhaime saying the Canadian government planned to freeze over $500 million in Libyan assets, which included sizeable payments owed to SNC-Lavalin. It was not Canada targeting SNC-Lavalin per se, but rather a general crackdown by authorities on major assets in the country, especially those that could be linked in any way to the government. The U.S. was putting the screws on the Gaddafi regime, and Canada had to follow suit. SNC-Lavalin was a large company, although $500 million was a pretty big knock by anyone's standards. So Duhaime called me to see if I could help.

At that time, I told him that I could never help in Canada or on Canadian issues. I was chairman of the Security Intelligence Review Committee and well connected in government, which was exactly the problem. The conflict of interest was glaringly obvious. I told him that they were on their own, and directed them to speak with Stephen Harper's chief of staff. That option must not have produced the desired results, because I heard from SNC-Lavalin again, asking if I could move the cash to Sierra Leone. It was possible, I said, although it required more than a few phone calls. And once I started talking to the relevant people, I could not stop the process. SNC-Lavalin would have to be 100 percent committed. There would be no going back.

We never got to that stage. Within twenty-four hours, the doors slammed shut, closing any sliver of opportunity that remained. I have no idea what happened to all that money. All of the executives I dealt with soon left the company. And I do not think most Canadians realized just how much SNC-Lavalin lost. Perhaps they got pennies on the dollar, but overall, the company took a massive hit.

SNC-LAVALIN'S CALL TO me that day at the Old Fort Bay Club was an act of desperation. I doubted that I could be of real help with Al-Saadi Gaddafi. Why would he listen to me about how to handle his father? I was flattered that Riadh thought I could be of assistance. It was an awkward moment, however. I looked back at my family eating lunch. Pamela was casting inquisitive looks in my direction. Riadh thanked me for trying and put the call on hold, and I waited for the leader of the Libyan army to pick up.

I had met his father a few times before. The last instance was at the African Union in Addis Ababa, the capital of Ethiopia. Once called the Organization of African Unity and now made up of more than fifty countries, it was somewhat the equivalent of the European Union. I thought Muammar Gaddafi was eccentric, polarizing and one of the few leaders who truly stood up for his country. He always looked at what he could do for Libya, as opposed to what was good for the rest of the world. I did not ascribe to all of his policies, of course, although I admired his willingness to stand up to the established world order.

At least in the beginning, he brought relative prosperity to the country. He helped support other countries in Africa that had difficulty finding financial resources outside of the International Monetary Fund, which tended to be quite restrictive in its criteria for lending.

Sierra Leone essentially depended on this assistance. After the civil war, resources and infrastructure had been almost completely destroyed. My homeland had never quite developed a system where the people benefited from its God-given raw materials in a tangible way. It became a breadbasket for other people. Militias, governments and corporations ripped out the diamonds without giving back to the country. Libya used to supply Sierra Leone with sizeable sums of money in support. It was important to the solvency of the country.

Gaddafi overstayed his welcome in Libya. What made him a great leader in his early years—passionate, uncompromising and ruthless—also made him a villain near the end. It was a story we saw many times in African politics.

Democracy, I believe, does not travel well to countries facing vast economic disparities, especially in places with established feudal or tribal areas. You cannot adopt democracy with a few ideas or a piece of paper. And you especially cannot do so with guns, bombs and troops on the ground.

Sometimes leaders who came up through the democratic process in Africa were actually worse, because it was a flawed process. Africa is evolving, and perhaps democracy will be the answer once the continent has had a few hundred years to get it right.

I heard shuffling. The cell phone was pressed hard to my ear.

"Yes? Porter?" Saadi said roughly.

"Yes, hello, Mr. Gaddafi. How are you?" I asked.

"We're in the middle of a war," he declared. "These rebels are slipping. We will get them in the end. I have no doubt we shall be victorious."

I hesitated for a moment, choosing my words carefully. "From what I have seen, it would be very difficult for you to win," I told him. "Have you ever thought about compromising?"

"Compromising? What do you mean?"

"You know the rebels will not accept your father's leadership."

"What are you saying?" he screamed. "I should turn against my father?"

"No, Saadi," I said, calmly. "I think you should be both his friend and his enemy. You need to be his *frenemy*."

I must admit I was thinking on the fly. I had not expected this call over lunch. Standing on that ridge, overlooking the ocean, I looked back at my family and was reminded of something one of my daughters said recently. She asked me if I had ever heard of the concept "frenemy." It was someone you would never deliberately hurt. You do not wish them ill. At the same time, you might need them for something important, and that could also make them your enemy.

It struck me as incredibly insightful, perhaps because I had so many "frenemies" in my life. I knew a great deal of people, some powerful and others not, cutting across continents, cultures and religions. Some were my "friends," in the sense that they could shake my hand, call me and meet me for dinner, and we might do business. But did I trust them completely? Would they stick by my side when the chips were down? Would they use me for their own benefit? Very few people would pass as real friends. But certainly, they were not enemies. In the end, perhaps they were better classified as "frenemies." It could be a powerful frame through which to gauge relationships, if you knew how to use it.

"I am not saying you should attack your father," I continued.

"Then what? I don't understand."

"You have to portray him as someone whose time has passed. You can step up to the plate, Saadi. There might be a small window of opportunity for people to retreat into their corners. You can still maintain a degree of loyalty."

Silence grew between us. Did I say the wrong thing? Had the call been disconnected? "Hello? Are you there, Saadi?"

"I will think about it," he cut in. "But I don't like the idea at all."

And then he was gone. Saadi handed the phone back to Duhaime, and he thanked me for speaking with him. I returned to my fish, now cold.

AS HISTORY TELLS us, Saadi did not take my advice, although the record shows that, in the month or so following, he did try and play the mediator, offering a more moderate line to the international community.

By then, however, bombs were starting to fall on Tripoli. Perhaps it was too late. I do think, though, that cutting out his father and trying to broker a new leadership was the family's best and only chance. Within a few months, the war was lost, his father was dead and Saadi became a fugitive in Africa.

It was also bad news for SNC-Lavalin. Libya cracked the whole can wide open, whereby all of their dealings became suspect and reviewed. And because of my close affiliation with them, my own credibility got dragged through the mud. Duhaime and Riadh would soon be shown the back door, shortly before being tied up in fraud charges over the $1.3-billion hospital contract in Montreal. The central leadership fell apart, and the company became the pariah for business in Canada. It was later reported, according to seized documents by the Royal Canadian Mounted Police at SNC-Lavalin headquarters, that Al-Saadi Gaddafi had received elaborate gifts from the company over the years in exchange for contracts. He was even offered a high-level executive position and $150,000 annual salary.

I could not speculate over whether those allegations were true. After all, I watched from the sidelines as the company struggled with these controversies.

What I can say, however, is that doing business in Africa and the developing world is never easy. It might seem trite or obvious to say so, but I think Westerners are somewhat naive on this point. They approach it with a kind of superiority and arrogance. Like the political landscape, and the struggle with democracy, these places cannot be judged within the same historical context.

Traditionally, business in the developed world is done by favours and relationships. Some would call it corruption; businessmen, politicians and other leaders in these countries would call it practical. Financial considerations for those who make the deal happen are also considered normal. Some favours are personal, while others are more for the masses. Some are both. I will give you a contract for that bridge, but you need to provide a water system for these villages. No doubt the villages need a new water system, and I will curry favour with the locals before the next election. That is how things get done.

Business is more informal. I once brought an Austrian company into Sierra Leone to discuss a particular mining contract. When I put the two parties together, they would not discuss business during the first meeting. Like I said, the developing world functions on relationships. The parties want to feel as if they know each other. And perhaps you could provide a favour to strengthen that relationship. In that instance, the first discussion was about bringing in schoolbooks for the local high schools. It was expected that both sides would get down to mining soon.

The Western world should take a step back before judging too harshly. The perception of corruption may simply be cultural. And the West is not so far removed from this way of thinking as some might like to believe. When I was in Britain, it was clear that the real business was not conducted in the boardroom. The old boys of Cambridge or Oxford would congregate in the clubs of London. In Detroit, I saw the inner workings of the "good old boys" approach first-hand as a member of the Country Club of Detroit and the Detroit Athletic Club, where movers and shakers played inside baseball. Favours and relationships in North America and Europe are alive and well, I can assure you. People have just got better at hiding it, or calling it something else. There is a veneer of transparency, with the rest driven by outside interests.

International business, however, was an entirely different proposition. In my day, most North American companies wanted to do business in the developing world, whether in Africa, Asia or the Caribbean, but had very limited success. They could not make the translation needed to seal the deal.

I found that companies quickly fell into one of three cat-
egories. The first were those that stuck a toe in the water and
jumped back squealing, complaining it was too hot. The
second were those that tried to impose their ethics and standards on the country. Sometimes it worked, but unless you
had a monopoly or superior technology and price point, it
was unlikely you would get the business. Emerging nations
had caught up considerably; you were competing against
China, India and other powerhouses. Even companies out
of places like Egypt and Nigeria could compete for some
projects. No, it was the third group that rose to the top.

When in Rome, we shall be Romans.

Companies that adapted and changed with the circumstances did very well. SNC-Lavalin, for example, created an
international subsidiary to do business in a way developing
nations could understand. If you looked at their portfolio, it
was incredibly successful in mining, dams, oil refineries and
healthcare systems. Much of this work in Africa improved
countries' infrastructures and created jobs.

I always believed that SNC-Lavalin was an excellent partner for the continent. They did business where nobody else
could. The situation in Libya was horrible timing. If the
civil war had never happened, SNC-Lavalin would still be
building there today. I maintain that it is one of the most
dynamic and worldly companies in Canada.

Meanwhile, as SNC-Lavalin fought for its reputation, I
had my own problems.

AMID ALL THIS turmoil, resentment lingered in Quebec
that this alien, this outsider, had swooped in, got the impossible done and now wanted to leave. Meanwhile, my international business dealings were flourishing. Perhaps, like

Icarus, I had flown a little too close to the sun. In hindsight, I can see that I should have stuck to my guns and resigned.

I could feel the ill will rising around me. And as time went on, my relationship with SNC-Lavalin was used as ammunition, causing my own armour to crack. I was attacked for perceived conflict of interest, even though my business dealings were overseas. Canada and Africa did not share many business relationships, and my own dealings there were enough to cast doubt on my integrity. Nobody dared say anything to me. It was all private talk, whispers at cocktail parties or around the water cooler.

And then, around three months later, on that dreary day in London, the big blow came when the *National Post* dredged up the arrangement with Ari Ben-Menashe—the fated deal that never was. My armour had been pierced, giving my critics the chance to deal a crippling blow.

After the *Post* article and my subsequent resignation from the Security Intelligence Review Committee, I had had enough of Montreal. It was becoming a free-for-all there. The vultures started circling. I was not having fun anymore.

So, on November 28, 2011, I wrote another letter to Senator Angus. This time, I would not be persuaded to stay on any longer:

> While some members of the Board of Directors and I have not always agreed over the years, we have always been in lock step when the best interests of the institution were on the line. Our success, and ultimately that of the MUHC, has been anchored by our ability to make difficult decisions. This should not stop. Unfortunately, even though the Board has expressed its support for me as CEO, I think it is fair to say that the relationship has

become more difficult and I'm not convinced that it will be possible for me to advance the institution's objectives in the short remainder of my term.

I suppose I did retreat to the Bahamas, but not out of guilt. I left the city that had begged me to stay while vilifying me at the same time. It was an appropriate ending to a situation that had felt confused from the start.

10.

FOUNTAIN
OF YOUTH

PETER NYGÅRD, ONE of the wealthiest men in Canada, sat across from me at a small table, the two of us tucked away, beyond prying eyes or cocked ears, in a remote meeting room on the lower level of the Bahamas' Sheraton Beach Resort, awaiting the prime minister of the Bahamas. Nygård's long, flowing greyish-blond hair hung well below his shoulders. His white shirt was unbuttoned halfway down his chest. He wore loose-fitting pants and slip-on shoes with no socks. Normally relaxed, talkative and gregarious, with a wide, crinkly smile, at this moment the multi-millionaire fashion mogul was furious. Things were not going his way. Hot, flustered and impatient, he bounced an ankle on one knee, mumbling about broken promises. Nygård and I were not alone. Beside me was Joy Jibrilu, a Bahamian who served as deputy minister in the Prime Minister's Office. Nygård had brought Kevin Klein, another Canadian and one of his top executives at Nygård Biotech, a new company focused on regenerative and stem cell therapies. We had been waiting for ten minutes or so, although Nygård's bad mood made it feel like hours. I thought he was going to burst.

Suddenly, a huge bodyguard opened the door and Prime Minister Perry Christie swept into the room, elegantly attired as always in a formal pinstriped suit. We all rose and he shook our hands. Nygård was not interested in ceremony.

"Why do you have me stashed in here, Perry?" he barked.

Christie stepped back. He looked surprised, but quickly recovered with a smile. "Please, everyone, take your seats."

Nygård returned to his chair but kept both eyes on the prime minister. Christie sat down at the head of the table and released a long breath.

"I have to deliver a speech in one of the conference rooms upstairs," he said softly, apparently answering the question, but not making eye contact with Nygård. He pulled out his cell phone as he spoke, appearing busy and distracted. A few seconds later he took out another phone and placed both on the table in front of him. "So I don't have much time, I'm afraid." He turned to me and smiled. "How are you, Arthur? Where are we at with things?"

I opened my mouth to speak.

"Do you intend on honouring our arrangement?" Nygård blurted out.

Christie raised an eyebrow. "Yes, I do, Peter. But as prime minister of the Commonwealth of the Bahamas..."

"Before the election," Nygård snapped, "we spoke about the stem cell bill being the first piece of legislation before the House of Assembly. Not the third. Not the second. The first. We are a week in, and I have heard nothing. You haven't taken my phone calls. I got a call back from one of your assistants. And now, instead of coming to my house, you have us meeting in some basement. So now I'm here. You're here. We're all here," he boomed, throwing his hands in the air. "So, please, you tell me, where are we at with things, Perry?"

I immediately knew that the meeting would not last much longer. Earlier that morning, Christie had called to ask my opinion on how to handle Nygård. He had been invited to his compound, otherwise known as Nygård Cay. "You are the prime minister now," I said. "So what if he donated large sums of money to your campaign? It would not look good to go to his home." I recommended he invite Nygård to his office, although clearly Christie opted for a different rendezvous that suited his agenda.

IT WAS MAY 2012. I had returned to my family's home in Nassau shortly after my resignation from McGill Hospital Health Centre in late 2011. As it turned out, I had plenty to keep me busy there.

The election campaign had ended only a week before. Christie and the Progressive Liberal Party won by a landslide, a two-thirds majority, over Hubert Ingraham and the ruling Free National Movement. On the day before the election, Christie looked awful. I sat beside him in his living room with a few other supporters. He was slumped on the couch in a yellow PLP shirt, eyes reduced to slits, half-listening to the last-minute advice being fired at him from all angles. Morale was low. Most people did not think he would win, let alone by a comfortable margin.

On election night, I went to the bar in the gated community where I lived, at Old Fort Bay, to watch the results rolling in. I sat there, drinking a glass of wine with a private banker, and it was apparent where the crowd's allegiances stood. They were wearing red, the colour of the Free National Movement. The only person wearing yellow was the bartender. And as the votes were counted, the bar got quieter and quieter. The place cleared out. Pretty soon it was just the bartender and me, smiling ear to ear.

The expatriate community, which tended to live in the high-end communities of Nassau, had put their weight behind the FNM. The PLP, by contrast, was considered a party of the people. Its slogan was "Bahamians first." It was also the party of the country's founding father, Sir Lynden Pindling, who formed the first government after the Bahamas achieved full independence from Britain in 1973. But as the Bahamas prepared to celebrate its fortieth year, paradise had been somewhat lost. In my mind, a government is responsible for only three things: healthcare, education and security. And this archipelago of around 350,000 people or so, only a couple hundred kilometres off the coast of the U.S., was failing miserably at all three.

While Nassau had a good private hospital and various specialty clinics in Nassau, the main public institution was out of the Third World. Security-wise, crime had never been worse. During the election, the PLP famously put up billboards revealing the record murder rate, which was far higher than those of many cities in North America with several times the population. It was a gutsy move, especially when the signs went up in areas frequented by tourists. Discontent was strong enough to warrant the risk. The gulf was growing between the rich and poor, literally. The bad area of Nassau, known as "over the hill," was actually on the other side of a gradual incline towards the centre of the city. Tourists would never go there. It suffered from routine shootings, stabbings and robberies.

Part of the problem was the country's drug legacy, which had flourished particularly during the late 1970s and early 1980s, when places like Norman's Cay became famous for funnelling drugs up through South America and into the U.S. But the cartels had mostly moved on. The U.S. cracked down on those activities, and trafficking had become far more complex. Much of the crime problem now came from poor education and high unemployment. Half the schools were derelict, without suitable teachers and supplies. Each year, the local newspapers would report on the countrywide averages in English and math. They were always appallingly low. In truth, many average Bahamians lacked basic literacy.

The same Bahamians worked as porters, waiters and housemaids in glistening resorts on white-sand beaches, if they were lucky. Times were tough following the financial crisis in 2008. People did not have money to travel like before, particularly people in America, where the majority of tourists came from. Tourism was the lifeblood of the economy, so all of society felt the pinch.

The PLP had promised change. It pledged to put Bahamians first once more. The FNM was the ruling party, and despite a loss to the PLP in 2002, it had ruled for fifteen of the last twenty years. Ingraham, or "Papa," as he was affectionately called, had become an icon of Bahamian politics. I suppose people simply assumed that his streak would continue. What they seemed to forget was just how disenfranchised the average Bahamian felt in 2012. On the night of the election, practically no one in that bar at Old Fort Bay was a registered voter. They were top executives, investors and perhaps permanent residents. But they had no direct say in the next government. The "real" Bahamians were living downtown in a crowded urban sprawl, where white people would never go, a place where the power and plumbing routinely cut out. So what if the FNM had built new roads in the capital? Most Bahamians do not own a car. Does it matter that we have a brand new airport? Most Bahamians have nowhere to fly to. They had had enough. They demanded change.

PERRY GLADSTONE CHRISTIE had served as prime minister from 2002 to 2007. Ingraham had ruled longer, but Christie was a familiar face. A bright man and a great thinker, Christie was also an excellent politician, and could win the election if the circumstances were right. His strongest attribute was the ability to be all things to all people, from bank presidents to citizens on the street. He could change his accent, his demeanour, even how he walked, to suit the situation. Every Christmas and New Year's, the Bahamas celebrates its largest cultural festival by shutting down the main thoroughfares of the capital for a parade. Teams spend months crafting elaborate and colourful costumes, and throughout the night they belt out music and perform choreographed dances. One year, the prime minister descended from his perch to dance with one of the teams, much to the delight of the crowd.

He and I first met back in 2000, shortly before his first term as prime minister, when I was first contemplating the Cancer Centre in Nassau. When I lived in Detroit, I saw Bahamian patients on occasion, and it was one or two in particular who convinced me to start a practice on the archipelago. I immediately hit it off with Conville Brown, a well-known cardiologist in the Bahamas, and we agreed to go into business together. I only agreed to launch a clinic in Nassau, however, if it was of such quality that treatment would be equivalent to that offered in centres in the U.S. or Canada. The Cancer Centre in the Bahamas became the first such Bahamian clinic to be accredited by the American College of Radiation Oncology.

But doing business in the Bahamas was not easy. The country has always been known for a laid-back attitude, the sun, sand and sea—a place where you can shed your watch and immerse yourself in island time. People are more than happy to take your tourism dollars, as long as you eventually get back on a plane. Investing and living in the Bahamas was another matter entirely.

Bahamians had a love-hate relationship with foreign residents. As the descendants of slaves, with an economy largely dependent on America, they were suspicious and fearful of neo-colonialism. The situation was made worse because the two groups rarely mixed. When foreigners set up shop, they tended to carve out enclaves and exist in their own little bubbles. It would be unusual for foreigners to have dinner parties with Bahamians. Similarly, Bahamians segregated themselves, and mistrust, greed, envy and jealousy prevailed. Of course, foreign investment was still well entrenched, and to an extent, outside business interests controlled the country. Bahamians could not stop foreign integration, so they expressed displeasure through bureaucratic and legal inefficiencies. Immigration, obtaining permits and opening a U.S. dollar account could be very easy, or extremely difficult. It was indeed possible to join the club, if you knew the rules.

I approached the challenge as I always did. I became one of them.

Christie was wary of me at first. A few years before, an oncologist from New York had set up a cancer clinic across the street from Nassau's main private hospital. He invested millions, said the right things and brought in all the right equipment, but as it turned out, someone failed to calibrate the machines properly. Patients got fried. A rash of Bahamians had suffered damage to their spinal cords, muscles and bones. The American investor hightailed it out of the country once patients started asking questions, and several years later you could still walk into the clinic and see all of the abandoned equipment. Even the patient charts were still attached to beds. This horrible experience had only intensified the Bahamians' natural suspicions.

As construction neared, I assured Christie that my clinic would be different. I was a noted oncologist with an impeccable reputation. I was a former president of the American College of Oncology, and it was my intention to certify the overseas clinic as quickly as possible. One reason, however, reassured him above all others—I was coming to the Bahamas to live.

It was around this time that Nassau became home for my family. My plan was not to make a quick buck and leave. I wanted to truly integrate myself into the society. I used to joke with Christie that Sierra Leoneans and Bahamians were not so different. Both societies came to be because of where the slave boats stopped. From the beginning I played upon these similarities and developed social linkages with prominent Bahamians, rather than joining a foreign clique.

I soon became a member of the New Year's Club, a group made up of wealthy black Bahamians who mostly supported the PLP. Every December 31, forty of us would spend the night together. Normally we held this event in a private room at one of the hotels in the capital, but one year, shortly before the 2012 election, a few of the members decided to switch things up. The Bahamas, and Nassau in particular, were home to a number of gated communities, although none of them rivalled Lyford Cay. This community in the western part of the island was probably the most exclusive, and mostly housed foreigners—wealthy businessmen, celebrities, developers and bankers. You might think that no locale would be off-limits to the New Year's Club, but in a country like the Bahamas, infiltrating Lyford Cay was a mission, and the New Year's Club undertook it as though we were bent on taking the country back. I remember quite well when the forty of us, with our wives, invaded the clubhouse for dinner that night. I can guarantee the other members milling around us had never seen so many black people in there at one time. One prominent attorney and politician poked me on the shoulder as we entered.

"Did you bring your passport?" he jested.

It felt as though we were entering another world. In fact, some members of the New Year's Club had never been behind those walls before. Nor would they go back. At Lyford Cay, our club could not shake the feeling of being in foreign territory. The following year, we returned to a downtown hotel.

In my mind, that night truly demonstrated the divide between white and black, foreign and domestic, which still exists in the Bahamas today.

Tough economic times only heightened the xenophobia among Bahamians, and certainly, it helped secure the PLP's victory in the next election. Bahamians, however, must eventually make peace with their place in the world. The country is and will always be a tourism hub. While it has a financial services industry, it lacks the space and natural resources to help spur true diversification. Meanwhile, the many Americans who flock to the Bahamas are finicky people who do not like stepping outside of their comfort zone if they can avoid it. So for them, the Bahamas feels like home. The country's currency is interchangeable with the U.S. dollar. People speak English and subscribe mostly to American values and pop culture. Any country that depends on a service industry will struggle with identity, with bending to others. This means the government must in-evitably pander to the foreigner. Just avoid being too noisy about it.

Soon, I was no longer seen as a foreigner. In addition to the Cancer Centre, I invested in other local businesses, such as a nightclub and a radio station. I bought and sold land. Christie and I became friends and confidantes. He called me about as often as I called him. If Christie had one major shortcoming, however, it was his inability to make decisions. He procrastinated on many things, waiting for the wind to blow in a certain direction and then following it. Often he was unable to make decisions in the healthcare field. We would talk about things and come to an agreement, but still fail to reach the finish line.

It was not a quality uncommon among politicians, although I would suggest he particularly struggled with it. To my mind, it was a big reason why he won elections and yet failed to hold on to power for a second term. After you spend so much political capital getting elected, you need to deliver on promises or cut those supporters loose. You really need to strategically deliver on promises. Christie, though, never wanted to disappoint people or end up on the losing side. He did not want to make enemies. But indecision can create enemies as well.

This shortcoming was what got him into trouble with Nygård.

HAVING WORKED CLOSELY with Christie, I knew that what Nygård said during that meeting at the Sheraton was true. Christie had pledged to bring stem cell legislation to Parliament very shortly after the election. Nygård wanted the prime minister to pounce. After such a resounding victory, he felt Christie should simply slip the legislation in right away. It would pass without a second thought, lost in the elation and white noise of an election. But the prime minister hesitated, and when he asked my opinion, I told him the truth: stem cells were too important, sensitive and controversial to introduce without careful consideration.

You couldn't just throw yourself into the business of stem cells. It would make or break the country's reputation as a hub for medical tourism.

Stem cell therapy has been around since the 1970s. Only in the last few years have stem cell research and procedures grown in sophistication and managed to find their way into mainstream medicine. In essence, cells found at the beginning of life have the ability to become any tissue in the body, whether in the brain, the leg or your big toe. As these cells become differentiated, or grow older and get assigned to specific areas of the body, they lose this ability. The medical implications of this basic truth are staggering. If the science could be perfected, with stem cells effectively replacing older ones, we would have the ability to treat and perhaps cure a variety of illnesses. Stem cells even have the ability to rejuvenate the body and make us younger. Traditionally, these cells were harvested from early abortions, or from in vitro fertilization, where a physician implanted five or six embryos, knowing only one or two would take and the rest could be shed for their cells. Another way was to simply get someone pregnant and remove the embryo before it reached the fetal stage.

Suffice it to say, all of these methods had generated considerable controversy in the Western world and prevented the therapy from firmly taking root. The Bahamas would be no different. It was a highly religious society. Bishops and priests had managed to ban the Hollywood film *Brokeback Mountain*—the story of two homosexual cowboys falling in love—from the country's theatres. Religious leaders tended to be kingmakers in any election, and the wrong decision could be political suicide. So I knew right away that, even though there was interest in establishing stem clinics in the Bahamas, these methods would never fly.

I advocated for two other techniques. The first was harvesting areas of the adult body known for having stem cells, such as the tissue surrounding the kidneys. These cells had potential, but nowhere near the potency of the real thing. The future, in my mind, was the re-engineering of normal cells. In other words, take cells from the arm and transform them using chemicals and other treatments so that they act and respond just like embryonic cells. Think of it like a computer: to get the performance needed, you hit the hard reset, taking cells back to a more primitive state. The science is getting there. One medication I took for my cancer, for example, acted as an inhibitor that reprogrammed my cells.

Even after you sort out the issue of harvesting cells, the treatment is still rife with controversy. Are humans meant to monkey around with our genetic makeup? I never put much stock in this argument. As with everything else, times have changed. If you had an infection one hundred years ago, odds are you would have died. We have a natural tendency to evolve and push our limits, and when that tipping point happens, science drifts into what seems, at the time, to be macabre.

Scientific innovation happens whether we like it or not. The real question is, can society balance innovation with reasonable, moral and altruistic practices? I believe we can. And I have often told critics that we are only at a primitive stage in the realm of stem cells. We will not be cloning humans anytime soon, or mixing the genetic material of leopards with humans to make us run faster.

We have not landed on the Island of Dr. Moreau quite yet.

I've always had a keen interest in and knowledge of stem cells. In the most basic terms, oncology deals with cells gone wrong, and potential therapies lie in the manipulation of cells to eradicate ailments such as cancer. And given our close relationship, Christie leaned on me from the beginning when it came to stem cells. He also saw the potential. In a country that lacks economic diversification, cutting-edge clinics could bring new-found prestige and investment to the archipelago.

It made sense on many levels. The Bahamas was an independent country and English-speaking. It was located just off the coast of the U.S., with plenty of flights to and fro on a daily basis. And it had a reasonably well-educated medical establishment. These factors added up to an opportunity to do something special, the chance to develop a framework for novel practices and research, if the right regulations and guidelines could be created.

The prime minister was also interested in stem cells for personal reasons. Christie was something of a hypochondriac. He was always worried about a cough here, an ache and pain there, so much so that he often used to call me for a random checkup, or perhaps a few words of reassurance over the phone. He was also terrified of heart disease and cancer. Stem cells offered hope and a release from his anxieties, although his interest in the science paled in comparison to that of Peter Nygård, one of Christie's largest campaign contributors.

Like Christie's, Nygård's interest in stem cells was also deeply personal.

I FIRST MET Nygård at a party on Nygård Cay several years before Christie's re-election. It was one of the most impressive and also strangest estates I had ever seen. After passing through a security checkpoint, I encountered ruins, temples and waterfalls, colourfully lit from unusual angles. Inside his home, trees sprouted from the floor and twisted to the ceiling like columns. It was a sprawling place, spread out in a series of buildings on a peninsula, and you felt as though you were on a movie set. That feeling was only reinforced by the legions of beautiful women swanning about the premises, most of whom found their way to Nygård's side.

I barely spoke with him that night. Hundreds of people were there. I remember him being loud, happy and the life of the party. Nygård's success in the fashion world had brought him power, and it was clear he enjoyed it.

I would not see him again until December 2011, a few months before the election. Christie wanted me to help with the impending stem cell program, and he also needed a trusted intermediary. Nygård had plenty of money and knowledge about stem cells, but he seemed to me to be borderline fanatical.

Stem cells were his obsession. Dying was not in his lifestyle plan. He once told me that he wanted to live forever, or die trying.

From what I observed, the seventy-two-year-old seemed to be essentially dedicating the rest of his life to pursuing and perfecting these treatments, with the end goal of building a clinic of his own in the Bahamas. He spoke at length about his travels to places in the Far East and Asia, where he studied stem cells and met physicians, some legitimate and others charlatans, while receiving a number of treatments along the way.

Nygård was a true believer. He claimed that he was the fittest he had ever been, and he did look much stronger than your average septuagenarian. He routinely worked out and played beach volleyball with his bevy of models.

Nygård's enthusiasm and support were helpful, but they came at a price: he needed to be front and centre. He wanted to be kept in the loop as much as possible. And he did not have intermediaries to speak to him, or for him. If a decision or a straight answer was required, it could only come from him. This meant a great deal of face time. And that placed the prime minister in an awkward position.

My job had been to keep Nygård in check, or at least try. But following the election, Christie had purposely distanced himself. He knew that the legislation could not happen as quickly as Nygård wanted. Cutting him off, however, completely thwarted Nygård's need for contact and first-hand information. This explained why he was so upset that day at the Sheraton.

Christie assured him that the government was working on it. And the two agreed that Nygård would present a formal paper on the creation of stem cell therapy in the Bahamas. When I received it a few days later, it was abundantly clear, in my view, that Nygård was dreaming. The paper proposed a plan and accompanying legislation that had been attempted by one of his friends in California many years before, without success. The proposal was to build an institute and form a board of directors that would approve any regulations surrounding the science, with Nygård, of course, as its chairman. He would be judge, jury and executioner. It never could have worked.

First off, such a deal would make the prime minister look as if he was completely bending to Nygård's will. There were questions of power and sovereignty for the Bahamas. Meanwhile, the clinic would be performing anything but routine treatments. The success or failure of stem cell therapy in the Bahamas hinged on balancing innovation with patient care. Without that balance, you risk quackery. In my opinion, Nygård was less concerned about the universal healthcare benefits and more focused on how he could extend and improve his own life.

The plan lacked true consideration and a common sense approach. Christie agreed with me, and asked me to commission a set of lawyers to craft a government paper on establishing stem cell clinics. The process would take time, a commodity that Nygård hated losing more than anything.

The fashion mogul started courting other statesmen with his proposal for a research and treatment facility. In

July 2012, he received a letter from Denzil L. Douglas, the prime minister of St. Kitts and Nevis. It read:

> The Government is committed to immediately embark on passing the relevant legislation to establish the appropriate legal environment so as to enable the relevant research and treatment facilities in the fashion that would accommodate the Nygård Institute for Regenerative Medicine in its plans to open up a new frontier in medical tourism.

Douglas highlighted heart and vascular disease; oncology and hematology; metabolic diseases such as obesity; degenerative diseases like frailty, osteoporosis, Alzheimer's and geriatric disorders; and even neurological conditions as areas of focus and research.

Nygård jumped at the opportunity and, because I was a friend of Douglas, invited me along for the ride to St. Kitts to visit the proposed site. Nygård owned a plane the size of a commercial aircraft, with his name branded across the hull. The interior was lavish, all done in blue and white with silver accents—and accessorized with beautiful women. Seven or so models accompanied us that day. It resembled a nightclub more than a plane. It even had a stripper's pole, which the models quite liberally made use of. More than once, Nygård retreated into one of the bedrooms in the back for periods of time. He was a truly remarkable man, incredibly smart and successful in business, who took what he wanted. Nygård knew when to buy and when to sell, and never mixed business with emotion. He did what was needed, at whatever cost, to get ahead and reach his end game.

We did not meet the prime minister that day. This first trip was more of an informal meet-and-greet, a fact-finding mission. We toured the proposed site with the deputy prime minister and a few other officials. It was enough to get Nygård excited, and shortly thereafter we returned to St. Kitts. This time, Douglas was waiting for us on the tarmac. The country showed considerable promise for Nygård. In the end, however, I think that his heart was set on the Bahamas. He had lived there for decades and invested major time and money into its economy. St. Kitts made some lofty promises, but for Nygård it would have meant uprooting and starting fresh.

And after all, the tiny island of Bimini in the Bahamas, just off the coast of Florida, was already associated with the Fountain of Youth. Juan Ponce de León, the Spanish explorer and conquistador, often referenced Bimini in his travels, with the fountain rumoured to exist in the shallow pools on the island.

Nygård would have to be patient. A month or two later, upon my recommendation, the prime minister asked the Ministry of Health to create the National Task Force on Stem Cell Therapy Treatment, with me as its chairman. Having lawyers draft a proposal was not enough. If the country was to move forward, it needed universal consensus and input from all segments of society, which was why the committee included physicians, lawyers and religious figures, covering the medicine, the law and the morality of it all. I doubt Nygård was terribly pleased, although it showed we were moving forward. I did have his interests at heart. In fact, while he was itching to be a part of it, I urged him to stay away, make himself scarce, because a public show would in no way benefit him.

As it turned out, it was already too late. We turned in our paper on stem cell therapy, paving the way forward on legislation and a regulatory framework. But the Bahamas is a small place. While it has all the trimmings of a sovereign nation, deep down it is a city, where everyone knows everyone else's business. In the summer of 2013, just as stem cell legislation reached Parliament, the opposition started attacking Christie, blowing the whistle on the party's close links with Nygård. In addition to Nygård's millions in contributions to the PLP, controversy grew regarding a leaked video showing future members of cabinet celebrating on Nygård Cay on the night of the election. Nygård could be heard saying: "We got our country back." The mudslinging got so dirty that Hubert Minnis, the leader of the opposition, was found in contempt during a debate in the House of Assembly over comments he made on the relationship between Christie and Nygård. Even with the threat of imprisonment, he refused to retract his comments. Parliament was ultimately suspended, and the stem cell issue was derailed as the political drama played out in the public sphere.

At the time, however, I was only vaguely aware of these spats. Ironically enough, as bureaucrats squabbled over this fountain of youth, I found myself fighting for my life.

IT ALL STARTED with a bad cough. It was December 2012, just days before Christmas, and I had some x-rays taken at my clinic in the Bahamas. The initial diagnosis was pneumonia, which seemed like a horrible affliction at the time. Nobody likes to be under the weather over the holidays. I started on a course of antibiotics, and while the cough continued, I started to feel better. However, as an oncologist, I was also curious. A voice nagged in the back of my mind:

Why did you get pneumonia in the first place? I decided to have additional scans.

As on any other workday morning, I had my two cups of coffee and took the usual route in to work. Once there, I lay down on the hard examination table and administered a CAT scan on myself, just as I had ordered for hundreds of patients over the years. I went through the motions as if it were an academic exercise. And then, looking at the scans, I saw it. Displayed on the bright, backlit screen was an ominous mass on the left side of the lung. A few scans later, I discovered that my liver lymph glands and even my bones were not normal. I knew it had already spread.

There is no typical response to finding out that one has cancer. I made a living breaking the news to people and trying to find ways to fix it. Some people cry uncontrollably. Others remain calm and ask questions, trying to understand it, and fight back tears as their eyes become red and glassy. As for me, I calmly removed the x-ray print and went to see my first patient. At least emotionally, it didn't hit me right away. I felt as though this had happened to someone else. There was a disconnect.

I greeted my staff on the way to the waiting room and exchanged the usual pleasantries. I carried on like everything was normal, because the fact is, I did not feel like I was dying.

But as I finished with my discussion with my next patient—a wonderful gentleman and philanthropist from Canada—my mind was thinking about the next steps. I stepped into Conville Brown's office and tossed the scan on the desk. By this time, he had been my friend and partner for over a decade.

"What is this?" he asked, stacking the scans in front of him.

"It's me," I said.

He raised his eyebrows and snapped the first scan above his head, holding it close to the light on his desk. I could see his face grow dark.

"Yes, it's a cancer." It was hard for me to get the words out. "And it has spread."

Conville was silent for a moment. He placed the scan back on the desk and nodded. "Well, you're the expert," he said. "What shall we do?"

The medical community in the Bahamas was small and tightly knit. It did not take long before we had a pulmonologist, cardiac surgeon and anaesthetist in the office—all worried. On the phone we had Karol Sikora from the U.K., an eminent oncologist and a big thinker who had an uncanny knack of simplifying and crystallizing difficult clinical problems.

I was diagnosed with having a poorly differentiated adenocarcinoma. It is a type of lung cancer found in non-smokers; I never smoked a cigarette in my life. It is not the most common lung cancer, but the scans revealed that I was already in an advanced stage. This type of cancer tends to grow more rapidly compared to other forms of adenocarcinoma, which means it can quickly take over the organs and move through the body. If you looked at the textbook, I literally had no more than nine months to live.

I had trouble accepting that prognosis. After talking about it with my family and looking at that dark mass a second, third and fourth time, I stopped expecting to see another name on it. I was in a position of knowing a great deal about my illness. That was good, but it was also not so good. I had always run my life at 150 miles per hour. Mortality had never been in question. I approached my cancer like any other challenge I'd faced, except that I can assure you, cancer placed them all in perspective. I had never had to battle something that was truly life-threatening.

I decided to perform the radiotherapy myself. My colleagues were on holiday, Sikora was in England and frankly, I am rather good at what I do. I sent the x-ray films to my colleagues in the U.S. and the U.K., just to make sure I was not over-treating, under-treating or making any other mistakes. We did that for most of our patients anyway, so why not for myself? It is always best to have another set of eyes and minds reviewing one's decisions. Of course, the irony of meeting my maker in this fashion was not lost on me. It was actually humbling in many respects. I quickly developed a heightened sense of empathy for my patients. I believe that I was always a good doctor, but I don't think I ever truly understood what my patients were going through. When they left my office, I did not follow them home. I did not witness the physical and mental turmoil that accompanies cancer.

I continued to see patients after my own diagnosis, but I also started on platinum- and Taxol-based chemotherapy given through an ingenious device—a plastic port that had been placed below my right collarbone, which allowed the drugs direct access to my circulation. I started chemotherapy in January and set my goal to work through the treatment.

That was not to be as easy as I thought. One day, I took a shower and saw hair around my feet. Other days, I had trouble breathing. I coughed up blood and felt sick to my stomach. Walking became difficult. I even had trouble thinking.

I always thought of myself as a good thinker, but the treatment made even that seem like a Herculean effort. My mind drifted in and out, and suddenly I found myself searching for my bed.

In February, after two full courses of chemotherapy, I repeated my scans and tests. The scans showed that although the lung was slightly better, the liver had become much worse. We decided to change my chemotherapy from standard medications to something more specialized. Over the last few years, cancer medicine has become personalized. What that means is that we now don't just say we are treating a lung cancer or even an adenocarcinoma of the lung, but we look for the molecular markers that make Jack's cancer different from Joe's cancer and use new drugs to target those differences. In my case, I had a marker known as ALK, which occurs in only 4 percent of people with my type of cancer. This discovery allowed me to try a new drug that had only recently become available. I took it twice a day, and the side effects were hellacious. Each dose, one in the morning and another in the afternoon, was followed by violent bouts of vomiting and diarrhea—a rather unpleasant combination.

I never fell into the trap of giving up hope. I must admit, however, that on some days I wondered just how much I could endure. I nearly reached my limit later that month. As a complication of the cancer, I developed swelling in my left leg. An ultrasound revealed a blockage in the vein from my foot to the femoral vein, which is the main source of blood flow from the leg. While it could easily have been treated with blood-thinner medication, the risk was a piece of the blockage breaking off and floating into the lung. Something like that could have killed me instantly. So I arranged for a surgical colleague to implant a mesh filter inside my body as a precaution. It was a relatively minor procedure.

I was on my way to the operating room when my receptionist at the cancer clinic tapped me on the shoulder. She said someone from the Canadian Broadcasting Corporation was on the phone. They wanted to know my response to the charges that had been filed against me in Quebec. Earlier that day, the Quebec anti-corruption squad had issued an arrest warrant for two senior SNC-Lavalin executives (Pierre Duhaime and Riadh Ben Aissa), a Montreal hospital executive (Yanai Elbaz) and me over an alleged $22.5-million fraud surrounding the construction of Montreal's megahospital. We were charged with pulling strings to ensure that the SNC-Lavalin consortium won the bid. The hospital project was believed to be at the heart of a corruption scandal whereby SNC-Lavalin paid off key executives to secure the lucrative contract.

In a way, I was flattered, if amazed, that authorities in Quebec believed I could help mastermind such a process, one that involved so many people and layers of government. To pull that off, my alleged co-conspirators and I would have needed wide-ranging powers and connections, and to be working at a level of corruption far deeper than could rationally be possible. Put simply, the alleged conspiracy was not only improbable—it was impossible.

That said, the charges were not altogether unexpected, because I had been targeted for so many things in Montreal. In late 2012, just after my resignation from the Security Intelligence Review Committee and around the time of my diagnosis, McGill University filed a lawsuit claiming I had skipped out on a low-interest $500,000 loan for my

Montreal house. Around $300,000 of that loan was still owing. I did owe the money. The university gave these loans to anyone who worked there, and the deal was that when you sold your house, you had to pay back the loan in its entirety. Unfortunately, that arrangement changed abruptly around the time of my resignation as chairman of the Security Intelligence Review Committee. The university wanted the money right away.

I had left Montreal without paying back the loan, sticking to my original arrangement. McGill did what they had to do and filed a lawsuit. In the end, I paid off the loan once my Montreal house sold.

The loan issue was just another aggravation during a very troubling time. Dealing with a terminal illness, absorbing the constant blows to my reputation in Canada and managing a series of successful international businesses, however, had pushed me to the brink. It was not the best time for bad news.

As to the fraud charges, perhaps what bothered me most was the conduct of the Canadian authorities. I found it appalling that I had to learn through the media that charges had been laid. I was never properly served by the Quebec anti-corruption squad. About two months after the first story broke, I did receive a letter from the squad, entirely in French. I never received a translation, despite my lawyer's request for one. Aside from that, I received nothing in the mail, nor did I get a phone call. In the weeks and months that followed, I never heard a peep from the Canadian police.

Meanwhile, the media helped fuel the perception that I was in hiding and somehow unreachable, as if my home in a well-known gated community in the Bahamas was surrounded by a moat and electrified fences. I had maintained a home in the Bahamas for more than a decade. My daughters went to school there. I had a standard mailing address, and more than one phone number. I was a leading physician and businessman within the Nassau community.

My profession and ownership of a state-of-the-art cancer clinic also made the Bahamas an ideal place for treatment. I could have received treatment anywhere in the world. I chose to have it in the Bahamas. In the coming weeks, newspapers and broadcasters would also cast doubt on my illness, referring to my cancer as "alleged" and highlighting the fact that it was self-diagnosed. Yet my cancer had been well documented by physicians throughout North America and the U.K., all of whom could confirm the diagnosis.

But I have a tough skin. If you worry about what people say or become overly concerned with pleasing them, your success will be limited. I have never played it safe. But there was something particularly insulting about the notion of faking lung cancer. I found those insinuations low.

I also found it baffling that Canadians were surprised or even critical that I had no intention of returning to Canada. At the time, my cancer was such that travelling would have been dangerous. But more importantly, the Quebec anti-corruption squad did not rank high on my list of priorities.

I KEPT MY head down and focused on survival—literally. My family and I carried on. I started to get a little better through March and April. In May, I went on yet another new drug that made me feel much better, although the sensation was deceptive. It gives you another four to six months of relative comfort, but the mortality rate remains about the same. The cancerous cells come back. The cancer actually learns to evolve and work around the medication.

However, I felt like a million bucks. My hair grew back. As my wife would say, I was back to being a pain in the ass. I started conducting business deals, I got my cancer centres running again and I spent more time with my four daughters. We actually started fighting on occasion—something we had never done before, because I was never home. I did not have many hobbies outside of work, although I loved cars. I had a black Mercedes in the garage. It was fifteen years old and had tagged along with me since my days in Detroit. It was an S-600 with a beautiful V12 engine. It was a real muscle car. The children had driven it around Florida, which was probably why it was in such a poor state. It was also the most impractical car I ever owned and often had problems.

I started working on it again. I wanted to get it back into running shape. Throughout my cancer, I never gave up. I needed to stay active and hopeful. I had to believe that, like the old Mercedes, I could be fixed.

11.

ANYTHING
IS POSSIBLE
IN LA JOYA

A GUARD GRABBED me beneath the armpit and tossed me into a seat. He chained my wrists and ankles together and then attached the chain to the side of the armoured bus. His face was hard and uncaring, just waiting for the slightest look or indiscretion to prompt him to plunge the butt of his machine gun into my gut. Not that I could entirely blame him. After all, this was a bus bound for hell, otherwise known as La Joya, one of the most notorious and aggressive prisons in all of Latin America.

I was soaked with sweat in my light-coloured linen suit. I tried to keep my eyes to the ground but could not help shooting the occasional gaze at the chained prisoners around me—men in shorts and flip-flops, some shirtless. I did not stare. Tattoos of women, weapons, skulls and unidentifiable symbols riddled their arms, chests and hands. I could see wounds and bullet holes on their bodies, some fresh and others healed. Their eyes appeared hardened, without care or compassion. As the engine roared to life and we made our way across Panama City, I was not sure if I would survive the coming ordeal.

It was the morning of March 31, 2013, and while I knew the danger ahead of me, being chained to a bus was still preferable to being in the downtown city jail. Amid the stench of clammy and unwashed flesh, I could now see trees, buildings and people between the bars on the windows as we drove out to La Joya.

For three long days I had been languishing in a holding cell built for seven or so people but containing at least fifty souls. I believe the exact number was fifty-one, including myself, because I used to count the rows of heads around me to pass the time. The holding cell was so jammed that we all learned to sleep standing up. It sounds impossible, but you learn to do it by the second day. If I was lucky, I managed to worm my way to one of the walls as a leaning post. Most of the time, however, I simply found myself wedged between two people, eyes flicking open and closed for a minute or two at a time. Three times a day, at feeding time, a guard threw a pail of slop and a few bowls into the cell. I never touched them. It was too hard to move. I was too upset and disturbed by the events that had befallen me.

Just a week earlier, on the evening of May 25, Adina, my second-youngest daughter and a practising lawyer in the Bahamas, had driven my wife and me to the airport from our Nassau home. The plan was to spend a few days in Antigua and Barbuda and meet with the prime minister regarding a new cancer clinic under construction. It was my latest medical project. After building the original clinic in Nassau, Bahamas, nearly a decade before, a few other doctors and I were expanding these state-of-the-art cancer clinics across the Caribbean. The vision was to have top-notch cancer treatment, equivalent to or better than what you would find in North America or in Europe, spread out among several island states.

Since the Cancer Centre in the Bahamas had become the first foreign clinic to be accredited by the American Society of Clinical Oncology, the rest of the region stood to benefit from improved care. One of the key developments that made this multi-state cancer centre concept work was a unique form of teleconferencing that allowed our physicians across the system to work together as a single department. We were slowly becoming one entity with a common goal, bound together across miles of ocean.

The clinic in Antigua and Barbuda was a key addition in terms of connecting the dots. You can only do so much remotely. I needed to get my boots on the ground, view the construction and feel the bones for myself.

It had been six months since I had been diagnosed with lung cancer. While my treatment was rough, and I certainly experienced my fair share of ups and downs, I had entered a rather euphoric stage. A few weeks earlier I had begun a new kind of drug that almost made me feel like my old self again. I was making deals, fielding phone calls and puttering restlessly around the house. I'd thought about travelling before, but I didn't want to be one of those people on the plane pleading for a doctor. I didn't want to be wheeled off the plane as two hundred people watched, wondering why I had got on in the first place.

Now that I was feeling up to it, nothing could have stopped me from a quick trip to nearby Antigua and Barbuda. I decided to bring Pamela along for the ride. After all, she was a trained healthcare professional. I packed a bag filled with medications, including my chemotherapy drugs, and brought an oxygen tank built into a bag that I could throw over my shoulder.

I would live to regret my decision to travel.

WE ARRIVED IN Panama in the late evening of May 26. My wife and I were groggy as we disembarked and headed towards immigration. The plan was to head straight for the hotel and get some sleep before we flew out to Antigua and Barbuda at noon the next day. But we did not get far. Shortly after disembarking the plane and entering the terminal, I saw a collection of uniformed people, arms crossed and eyes narrowed, staring right at me and my wife. They knew we were coming.

At least a dozen officers from Interpol and other agencies seized our passports, and we were escorted to a holding area. When we got to a nondescript room, four blank walls closing in around us, they explained why I had been detained. Of course, I already knew the reason. Although I had never been properly served with the charges, and no officers had bothered to come see me in the Bahamas, the relentless press coverage was enough. I was the fifth and final suspect, the mastermind no less, in the alleged $22.5-million fraud concerning the Montreal mega-hospital.

I always knew I might experience some friction while travelling. But I had done nothing wrong. Meanwhile, my status as an ambassador-at-large for Sierra Leone, and the fact that I travel on this passport, provided me with protection. And I was right. Shortly after entering that holding area, I was released and waiting for our bags. But Pamela, my wife of more than thirty years, was held.

I had no idea why they were holding her. She had never been served with any charges. I called my daughters in the

Bahamas and the U.S., frantically asking them to call our lawyers and find out what was happening.

With bags in hand, I started pacing through the airport, tired and confused. Should I wait at the airport? Or carry on to the hotel? In the end, I figured it was best to head for the hotel. I did not know if, when or where she would be released. But if she did get out, the only logical place for us to meet would be at the hotel. It was just a stone's throw from the airport.

I hailed a cab, checked in, turned off the lights and tried to sleep. I lay on my back and just stared at the ceiling and into darkness. It had been more than three months since the arrest warrant had been issued in Canada. After the initial blitz of stories and accusations came a period of relative calm. I was so focused on my cancer, trying to get better and spending more time with my family, that it almost seemed as though the Canadian issues had gone away.

But there I was, alone, lying in the dark, and my wife was missing.

Time crawled by. After a couple of hours I couldn't take it anymore. I got dressed and headed back to the airport, but again she was nowhere to be seen. Nobody could tell me where she was. Feeling utterly helpless, I returned to the hotel and waited. Several hours later, I heard from my lawyers and the counsel general for Panama in the Bahamas. They called to confirm that Pamela had been detained on an international arrest warrant, charged by the Quebec anti-corruption squad with laundering the proceeds of crime; in other words, the millions I had allegedly received for awarding SNC-Lavalin the hospital construction contract.

At around 8:30 AM the text messages started flying.

"Dad? What is happening?" Adina wrote.

"Mum arrested," I wrote back. "What should I do?"

"Leave," she said. "Get out." Was that legal advice? Or was it the reaction of a concerned daughter? I wasn't sure.

My connecting flight, previously booked, was not until noon. I knew that authorities would be looking for me at the airport. I was trapped and cornered. The worst part, however, was that my wife had become implicated in these charges. Was she being used as bait or emotional blackmail? Even if the charges did not stick, the situation was now astronomically more complex. Pamela never wanted any of this. She never even moved to Montreal when I took the job at the McGill University Health Centre. Throughout my career, my wife preferred to remain in the background, content to raise our four daughters while I battled away on the front lines. She was a quiet and reserved person, and the fact that she was detained ripped me up inside.

My daughter was correct. Staying in Panama would not help my wife one bit. We would most certainly be detained in separate quarters. And given my medical condition, it was best to make my escape to a place where I could continue treatment while also handling her case with the lawyers.

I was packed and ready to go. Win or lose, I was going to make a break for it to Antigua and Barbuda, in the hope of staying one step ahead of police. Just minutes away from leaving, I heard a pounding on the door. I did not have to look through the peephole to know who it was. Instead, I grabbed my BlackBerry from the foot of the bed.

I texted my daughter: "They have come for me. You are in charge now."

"I love you," she wrote. "Who should I contact?"

"Obi, Conville, Gordon and Karol," I frantically typed, not bothering with full names as the pounding grew louder. She knew who they were. They were my lawyers and colleagues, and they were my close friends, people I trusted. They needed to know what was going on. I would need all the help I could get.

I would speak to Adina one more time before boarding that bus to La Joya. Shortly after Interpol and the RCMP questioned me and before they threw me into that downtown jail in Panama City, I told them I wanted to call my lawyer, and I called her. But really, I called to tell her I was sorry. When I heard her voice, I burst into tears, apologizing for imposing this hardship on the family. I was mostly sorry, though, for Pamela. We were in the same building but kept in different rooms. My daughter told me that it would be okay. She would begin researching lawyers and ask Panama's consul general in the Bahamas for recommendations. I had no idea who to hire. I did not know anything then.

I FOUGHT BACK the same tears on the way to La Joya. I hoped my wife was making out better than I was. Over the last several months, I had been hauled through the mud by the media and those I once considered my friends. Everything had been thrown at me, including doubt as to whether I even had cancer. A sadness and bitterness were growing within me. Was this really justice? Was this the law? For three months, authorities in the Bahamas could have questioned me. They could have filed a formal request for extradition. And now, to top it off, I had to worry about my wife's well-being, although, as the high, steel gates parted at La Joya Prison, my thoughts soon turned to my own survival.

The armoured bus ground to a halt in the centre of a courtyard. One by one they unlocked us from the side of the bus and we formed a line outside. We marched across the dusty courtyard, shuffling in our shackles at gunpoint, until we reached a small administration building. There was not much to do. I would imagine La Joya is less bureaucratic than prisons in the First World. They had already taken all of my things, so all that was required were a few signatures. I did not understand any of the paperwork because it was written in Spanish. Then the guards looked me up and down and signalled for me to take off my clothes. I later discovered from other inmates that the guards were looking for tattoos or other distinguishing marks to remember me by in case I was killed and disfigured. That was reassuring. I did as asked, shaking. I was so scared that I felt sick to my stomach. Within minutes they led me back into the courtyard. The guards escorted me to my assigned cellblock with machine guns digging into my back.

I could see faces peeking through a small window on a steel door. Not whole faces, just crazed eyeballs and sections of unshaven chins and cheeks. I was about to be tossed into hell. We stopped right in front of the steel door and the guards released the chains from around my wrists and ankles.

Without ceremony, the door was thrown open as if it were the emergency hatch on an airplane plummeting from thirty thousand feet. With one big push, I was sucked into La Joya Prison and the door slammed behind me. It was a melee of flesh, men packed on top of men, with the only light trickling in from small, barred windows. No guards were in sight. Instead, as far as the eye could see, a sweaty stew of hardened criminals looked me up and down in my soiled white suit.

La Joya Prison was built for around 240 people. Much more than double that number lived in the prison, and as a result, the dim, concrete corridors are highways of half-naked bodies. Vermin squeak and claw across the floor, chased by stray cats and dogs. The prison is shaped like a large rectangle, with a main corridor wrapping around the outskirts. Within, a single passageway leads to the cell-block, also rectangular, with cells on either side facing outwards. The inner hallways are dark and narrow. None of the cells are locked. The prisoners roam where they please, and indeed, space within a cell is a status symbol.

As I entered the corridor, dozens of men were sleeping on the floor or huddled into corners. On the far side of La Joya was the gym, and the lion's share of inmates slept there or on the false roof above it, which acted as a kind of loft space. Nothing was on the concrete walls except the occasional window with lines of string hanging from its bars, suspending underwear, shorts, shirts and other pieces of laundry. A basketball net hung from the gym wall, but nobody used it; too many people were sleeping on the floor.

The prison is a raw portrait of humanity. It is kill or be killed. Natural selection is the order of the day and only the strongest survive.

From the moment I arrived, prisoners began sizing me up on where I would stand in the pecking order. New inmates were a source of suspicion and fascination. The vast majority of prisoners at La Joya were Colombians, followed by Venezuelans, Mexicans, Panamanians, Jamaicans and other nationalities scattered here or there. Large portions of them had been arrested for drug smuggling, murder or rape. Make no mistake, these prisoners were the worst of the worst, divided into gangs throughout the prison, and so dangerous that guards would not dare walk among them.

You used instinct in the beginning. You worked off hunches, body language and appearance. The little things were of grave importance at La Joya. All you had were the little things, such as where you sat, how you looked at people and what trinkets belonged to you. Everything denoted status.

The corridors were so crowded that how you gave way to someone coming in your direction became very important. It was important not to show weakness. At the same time, failing to show respect to certain inmates may cost you your life. At first, you never really knew exactly how to respond. As I said, it was instinct. You rolled the dice and prayed that you did not come up with snake eyes.

My focus at first was to simply remain calm and meet people who spoke English. I would say only 5 percent of inmates fall into this category, which immediately made me stand out. Word got around, and certain people began to gravitate towards me. Prisoners want to know what you did on the outside. And they want to know what you can bring to the table on the inside.

There are carpenters, plumbers and masseuses in La Joya. During the day, many of the cellblocks become a lively marketplace where you can buy and trade just about anything, from fruits, vegetables and meat to cigarettes, drugs and alcohol, to cell phones and laptops. There are barbers, cooks and servants. I saw a man pushing an ice cream truck while clinking a tiny bell.

The guards are easily corruptible, and just about anything goes at La Joya as long as you have skills, social standing, the gift of the gab and, most importantly, money.

La Joya is not a prison. It is a self-sufficient town, a community unto its own, filled with hardened criminals who stick to a set of rules, regulations and creeds. It is a cross between *Lord of the Flies* and an underground post-apocalyptic civilization that has somehow adapted to survive. And as I wandered La Joya in those first few hours and spoke with the people there, it soon became clear what I needed to do. I started to look past the scarred faces, the muscles and tattoos, and the knives and guns tucked into the fronts of shorts. More was going on than just raw humanity. Just as I had done all my life, I started to move through the crowd and network. Most people I'd met in life were snakes, although they tended to wear different clothing. At least these men wore a snake's scales.

My first break came when I met a pilot from Colombia who spoke decent English. He was dark-skinned, medium height and build, and he did not have a single visible tattoo. My ears immediately perked up when he told me he used to work for Pablo Escobar, the notorious Colombian drug dealer. The pilot had been in La Joya for eight years after his plane, carrying a big payload of drugs, crashed somewhere in Panama. He seemed to be a prisoner of moderate standing. It was a good start, I thought. I went on to tell him that I was a businessman and doctor on the outside. The latter seemed to pique his interest.

Medical care in La Joya was nonexistent. A rudimentary clinic was located somewhere on the prison grounds, but it was not the kind of place you wanted to go to for treatment.

The equipment was archaic and the staff uncaring and borderline incompetent. As with the guards, interaction between inmates and staff was kept to a bare minimum. Meanwhile, if you happened to get sick or receive injuries during the night, nothing could be done until morning. You would literally perish on the concrete floor. So my position as a doctor placed me in high esteem.

Even if I had not been a doctor, I believe that my survival skills and ability to network and relate to people would have boosted me up the ranks. It was not the sole reason for my survival there, but it certainly helped. My greatest attribute, as it had been all my life, was the capacity to change the environment to suit my needs, rather than let the environment change me.

The pilot asked me to join him in his cell. That single request immediately vaulted me into the ranks of top inmates at La Joya Prison. Only around one hundred prisoners out of more than five hundred had access to a cell. When I arrived, seven or so people had created a life for themselves in a tiny concrete room. Curtains sectioned off each corner and space of wall. I could tell people were behind them by the sounds and shadows. The pilot walked up to the curtain in the right corner and whispered something in Spanish. Within moments, a large Colombian with tattoos splashed across his arms and chest swished back the curtain. I would soon learn that he was the big dog, so to speak. Every cell and every cellblock had one. This big dog was someone fairly high up in a Colombian drug cartel, and he happened to have been riding in the back with the drugs when the pilot's plane went down eight years ago. He also spoke English. I shook his hand and explained that I was a doctor.

My status in La Joya Prison was affirmed. I slept on the floor that night, but this cell was my new home. The pilot allowed me to use his cell phone to contact my daughters in the Bahamas and the U.S. And when I rose the next morning, I was a new man at La Joya. Nobody knew my name. I became known simply as "the doctor." My next task was to develop my living quarters. Once I was identified as an individual of skills and means, I had access to a whole army of workers ready to do my bidding. I commissioned the resident carpenter and craftsman to make me a bed. It was built so I could convert it into a desk during the day. I ordered sheets, pillowcases, a chair, a fan, some curtains and a lamp. I spoke with inmates with good access to the guards, and through them I had all of my confiscated things returned to me, including my medications and chemotherapy drugs.

In prison, you also develop a keen sense of conservation. Everything is valuable. String, for example, is a particularly sought-after commodity. It allows you to hang curtains and laundry. My fan had to be stabilized with string so it blew on me while I slept. Plastic bags. Electrical tape. Every item was useful and important. I bought a new BlackBerry and reacquired my iPad. Internet access was available through a fairly weak dialup connection.

I accomplished some of these feats through favours, connections and trade. Sometimes it was simply cold, hard cash. The prison possessed its own micro-economy. One inmate, known as "Western Union," could perform electronic bank transfers and cash withdrawals. He would take around 10 percent for his services, so a $1,000 withdrawal, for example, would give you $900. It was a steep tax to be sure, but like anything else in life, it came down to supply and demand. No automated banking machines were readily available, if you know what I mean.

Meanwhile, some inmates lent directly to the prison population, and while I considered entering this business, I decided against it in the end. Loansharking, so to speak, required more than just money in La Joya. You needed enforcement, or muscle, if and when clients could not or refused to pay.

I opted for the pawning and bartering business instead, which also proved lucrative. I was a businessman through and through. I thrived wherever I found myself, and hard time in a Central American jail would not stop me.

In this business, I simply allowed inmates to use possessions as collateral for short-term loans. For example, a fan was a desired commodity in La Joya because it was always sweltering. If a fan was worth $50, I would give the client $20 in cash. He would have one week to pay me with interest, which would come out to around $25, representing 25 percent return. However, if he could not pay me, I did not have his kneecaps busted. I kept the fan, which was worth much more than the loan in the first place. It was a win-win situation, and the business thrived.

It was not the Four Seasons, but life in La Joya could be expensive if you wanted the finer things in life. The business financed what I considered to be a tolerable lifestyle. I had two or three young men who walked around the cells with merchandise, calling out prices and selling these repossessed products. Everything in La Joya had at least a 20 percent markup. Four oranges, which might cost the average inmate a dollar, would be fifty cents on the streets of Panama City. My business of dealing with items already in the prison did not involve the logistics of smuggling or big markups. It kept things simpler. The products were already part of the micro-economy.

IT SOON BECAME clear to me that anything is possible in La Joya Prison if you are smart, possess a skill and know how to network. Life does not stop in prison. The prominent inmates have access to every mode of communication, so a great deal of time is spent conducting business. Many of the inmates were already connected through drug cartels, although new faces were always arriving as well. New deals and connections were struck. Just as I was quickly identified as a doctor, discovering the leaders of various drug cartels was not difficult. The hierarchy slowly presented itself. It flowed naturally. These men formed much of the prison's leadership, and it went down from there. At the bottom were the men who carried drugs, known as mules. At La Joya, they often became servants who washed clothes, delivered messages and ran errands.

Many of the cartel kingpins were my patients, which only boosted my profile and prestige. Within a week or two of my arrival, I had carved out a relatively comfortable life for myself in La Joya. On a typical day, I would rise at 6:30 AM, take a shower and convert my bed into a desk. For the next thirty minutes or so I would go online through my iPad, check email and read up on what was happening in the world. By 7:30 AM, Julio, my Venezuelan cook, would show up with my coffee, just in time for my online Spanish lesson. I made a point of learning the language so I could properly converse with my brethren. As when you're dropped in a foreign country, you pick it up quickly. By no later than 8 AM, I would get dressed in shorts, flip-flops and a T-shirt, grab my medical supplies, and do "rounds."

I always had a variety of cases to deal with. With drugs and alcohol so prevalent at La Joya, fights, skirmishes and stabbings were frequent. Sometimes new injuries were inflicted, while at other times old gashes or bullet wounds were causing trouble or discomfort. Fortunately, I had been travelling to Antigua and Barbuda with a well-stocked bag of medications and drugs, given my own condition. I made a point, however, of ordering basic drugs and equipment through my various connections so I could remain effective in my new-found role. Nevertheless, the situation did require some creativity on my part. I learned to remove stitches quite efficiently with a nail clipper. One patient had a swollen and infected molar, which I removed with a pair of pliers. Traditional anaesthetic was difficult to come by, but I had ready access to cocaine, which was used as a painkiller before it became a recreational drug. I took a dab of cocaine on my finger and rubbed it on infected gums, reducing the blood flow, numbing the spot and giving the prisoner a bit of a euphoric feeling. Not every case was so exciting. I also dealt with the usual ailments that we all tend to get, such as chest pains, colds, fevers, infections, stomach problems and pneumonia.

By 11 AM I would meet Julio back at my desk. We would discuss what I would like to eat that day—perhaps chicken in an orange-based sauce, washed down with a glass of dry red wine. I was told the wine was made in-house by a Nigerian inmate. I did not ask to see where or how he made it, but I had no reason to doubt it. Given how La Joya functioned, nothing surprised me anymore.

In the afternoons I took advantage of outdoor time. I wandered through the yard for two or three hours, speaking to people and networking. Later in the day, my friend known as "the Mexican" came by my cell for my one-on-one Spanish lesson.

Some nights, nothing happened. I would lie awake at night and hear strange sounds, clanking here or there, howls, inmates talking and sometimes screaming. Other nights were filled with activity. Occasionally my cellmates and I would watch the Panamanian soccer game. Around two weeks into my time at La Joya, a Colombian pop singer arrived at the prison. Apparently he had been found carrying a huge quantity of drugs.

I had no idea who he was, but judging by the wild mob, he was a bona fide celebrity in his homeland of Colombia. On Father's Day, the gym at La Joya was cleared out for a one-time concert. The prisoners constructed a stage at the front of the gym and brought in speakers and a microphone. It was a captive audience, so to speak. Every inch of that gym was packed with cheering, stomping, dancing and clapping inmates, perhaps thinking about life before La Joya. It was enough to make you forget about your situation, if only for a moment. It was a pop concert in every sense of the word.

At La Joya, life continues in such a way that you sometimes forget where you really are. However, it does not take much to jolt you back into reality. Violence occurs on a daily basis. The inmates are often bored, drunk or high on drugs. Most of the altercations are little skirmishes, although on occasion one or two men are killed or succumb to some kind of illness or injury. On the whole, however, there aren't too many power struggles. La Joya is remarkably well organized. Most inmates find their niche and role. Sticking to that role and remaining consistent and loyal to your group is paramount. Your word is everything. In that sense, prison life sometimes feels very predictable. If you buy a pineapple on credit from a merchant, always make sure you pay him. Never take something that is not yours. La Joya is the kind of place where you can leave your valuables in plain view. It is unlikely someone will take anything. But on occasion it happens.

I recall one incident where an inmate in the cell next to mine took a cell phone off someone's bed. The prison is such a small place. Everyone knows each other's business. It was not long before they found the thief, hauled him into the corridor and beat him close to death. They must have decided to give him another chance, because I was then asked to treat him. There are really only two punishments in La Joya: a severe beating or death.

Still, as predictable and organized as prison life can be, a lot of volatile people are at La Joya, and it could sometimes feel like a game of Russian roulette. You never knew the mood of the man next to you. Many of the prisoners are violent by nature, desperate, with nothing to lose, so it is essential to keep your wits about you and play a smart game. I tried to steer clear of politics and personal gripes. You also have to be careful how inquisitive you are. I never carried a weapon. I was content to simply be "the doctor," picking my spots and wielding power with my mind instead of my fists.

On June 19, nearly three weeks into my time at La Joya, a major fight broke out a few cells down from me. I heard it, but did not see it. I only saw the streaks of blood on the floor after the injured were dragged off. I never found out if anyone died. All I know is that several prisoners were stabbed. One was shot in the chest. I was not asked to provide medical care, and I was glad for it. Such incidents happened on occasion, but they were not routine.

Within hours of the incident, a bush telegraph spread through La Joya that a prison-wide search was coming. The guards had to at least give the appearance of authority.

Not a single prisoner was caught with his pants down. We had several hours to hide our contraband. The water system in La Joya had long been taken over and manipulated by the prisoners, so open drains, pipes and overturned tiles or stones were popular hiding spots. I had people in my cell take care of the hiding for me. You did not bother with items such as furniture, food, cigarettes or other everyday items. What guards were really looking for were weapons and communication devices. Of course, they knew these things were common within La Joya. If they happened to find your things, you always had the option of buying them back later in the day.

On June 20, one day after the shooting, we were all ordered into the courtyard. About four hundred officers arrived by bus and spilled into the prison. The place was trashed by the time they were done. In a way, the guards are more dangerous than the inmates.

Apart from the searches, the only time you see guards is during the "counting." Once a week, every prisoner at La Joya has to file into the courtyard to be accounted for. Beneath those massive walls, you can feel very small and exposed. Barbed wire adorns the top, and every few hundred yards is a lookout post containing snipers.

Typically, about two hundred guards are at the counting, carrying machine guns and appearing nervous, jittery and fresh-faced. These Panamanians are young men, practically babies, because working at La Joya is not exactly the best job in the world. Many of them make very little money, leading to ample bribery and contraband. It is also an incredibly dangerous profession. There is a reason guards never venture inside the prison. The inmates despise them. As we would march into the yard, hardened criminals would spew insults and taunt them, or even brush shoulders and touch them. The prisoners have no fear or inhibition. It is a semi-stable state that seems ready to explode at any moment. I was told there had been incidents when an inmate went too far, or a guard was pushed over the edge. And when one guard shoots, everyone shoots, including the prisoners.

The counting takes a long time. Or perhaps it just felt that way. It might be an hour or two before I would hear my name called over the mega-speaker. Then I could re-enter the prison. For me, the counting signified yet another week at La Joya Prison. It was one way that I marked time.

You never know what could threaten your survival. Sometimes it is the most basic of things. The water supply, for example, is not based on modern plumbing. La Joya is very much off the grid, so we depended on rainfall, which circulates through a twisted maze of pipes that have been diverted by the inmates. For a dollar or two you can have your water brought to you each day. A long drought, however, means the population could wither and die, although not before descending into violence and anarchy.

Those of us lucky enough to have a cell kept a bottle of water hidden for emergency purposes. It came in handy more than once. I remember during one stretch there was no water in the prison for three days. I used my reserves sparingly, and by the end of the third day, there were rumblings of a riot. But on the morning of the fourth day, rain fell from the sky.

As I came to realize just how cut off we were from society, I carried on and made my own way. As a sign of goodwill, I arranged for the delivery of some concrete, bricks and tiles so my cellblock could rebuild the shower and washroom facilities. I found it quite amazing just how self-sufficient we really were. There was no real public or government involvement at all, apart from keeping us within these walls. We were held in this place, but we managed it. I often heard the sound of jackhammers and electric saws down the corridors. At first, you might have thought a group of inmates was trying to escape. What they were really doing was making improvements to public infrastructure and living quarters. I have often thought that some of the inmates were vying for their cell to be featured as a centrefold in *Cells Monthly*.

A few weeks into my time at La Joya, I met an inmate from the Dominican Republic, in his late forties, who had been incarcerated for about ten years. He was due to be released in a few weeks. I remember talking to him about his role within the prison. He had carved out a very clear profession for himself as a craftsman. It was a task he felt comfortable performing in La Joya. He told me that he had no idea how he would fare in the outside world.

Here, he had friends and a purpose. His days were relatively predictable and his needs were more or less met. While it was amazing to even consider, the world out there had grown more daunting than La Joya.

But I never thought that way, even when weeks turned into months. Not even for a minute. I found my way at La Joya, but I kept my eye on the prize. I met with my lawyer, Ricardo Bilonick, every two days. We discussed our legal strategy and the road ahead. It was decided early on that it would do me no good if I were extradited to Canada. I would never see Pamela.

She had been forcibly extradited back to Quebec just a couple of weeks after we were arrested. Granted, she initially did not fight the extradition order. On the morning of the extradition, however, she had a change of heart. Pamela feared that she would be held hostage, used as the ultimate bartering chip to force my own extradition back to Canada. Her original agreement to voluntary extradition was revoked, using the same form provided by the Panama Foreign Ministry, and it was properly filed at the corresponding office on June 11. For whatever reason, it failed to sway the Canadian authorities. I was not there, of course, but Ricardo later described his utter shock when he received a call from one of Pamela's cellmates, a Canadian to boot, informing him that my wife had been picked up, kicking and screaming, for extradition. Ricardo was shopping at the time. He dropped his shopping basket in the aisle and sprinted for the car. But when he arrived at the airport, the authorities denied him access to Pamela. He was too late. My wife was off to Canada.

The Quebec anti-corruption squad set her bail at $250,000, among the highest, if not the highest, in its history. She had to surrender her passport and check in with police twice a week, and she was forbidden from contacting me or leaving the province of Quebec. Pamela was but a small piece in an alleged case of multi-million-dollar fraud. The agenda at play was clear. No, I did not want to be sucked into the trap that had been laid before me. I decided that I would fight extradition and the legality of my arrest as a Sierra Leonean diplomat. Many people questioned why I would ever choose to languish in La Joya rather than be hobbled back to Canada in chains. Those people don't know me at all. I had my reasons, which I will explain in due course.

Admittedly, my health was an ongoing concern. I continued taking my chemotherapy drugs. My mood and energy remained relatively high despite the cancer festering in my body. I had my oxygen machine. While my physician was initially denied access to me in the beginning, he made the trip in late June after my connections reached maturity. He brought me more medications and looked me over. But given the nature of my disease, what I truly needed was radiotherapy to the chest. I just tried to hang on, day by day, and hoped that the lawyers did their job—and did it well.

While I fought constantly for my release, I understood where my Dominican friend was coming from. I also came to depend on many prisoners. My cook, Julio, faithfully brought my coffee, lunch and dinner at the appointed time. When I provided a service or favour, it was repaid somewhere down the line.

I have found more honour in there than I have on the street. The code of conduct is so engrained, partly out of fear, but mostly from necessity. People look at you with a clear expectation. There is very little backstabbing, and when it occurs it is met with brutality. I suppose, as in *Lord of the Flies*, there is a constant tug-of-war between common good and self-interest. If one gets pulled too far in the latter direction, it unhinges the entire society. The only difference, however, is that no parents or naval officers will come to the rescue, no matter how many fires we light or how high and fiercely they rage.

We would all be left to burn.

WHEN I FIRST arrived, I thought it would be the worst experience of my life, and perhaps even my last. The conditions are horrible. For the vast majority of the inmates, the best they can hope for is to stay alive, with cold concrete for a bed. I have seen men beaten, bloodied and even killed right before my eyes. But at its heart, La Joya Prison is not so different from a boardroom or parliamentary caucus.

If my experience in La Joya proved anything, it was the ubiquitous power of negotiation.

I have done it at the very top and the very bottom.

12.

CHEATING TIME, DOING TIME

WHEN I FIRST started my career as an oncologist, most cancers were death sentences. The prognosis was fairly accurate. If the doctor said you were going to die within a year, the odds were you would. Fewer treatments, therapies, drugs and solutions were available than we have today, and I spent much of my life trying to change that. I never thought I would be a living embodiment of this work.

By October, I had survived six months of hell in La Joya Prison. It had also been around ten months since the diagnosis, and considering I'd been given no more than nine months to live, I was already cheating time—while doing time. A big reason for that was my remarkable reaction to a set of cutting-edge drugs. I have my friend and mentor Karol Sikora to thank for that. I was responding, keeping the cancer at bay, but more than that, I had refused to accept my fate. Stubbornness can be a powerful drug.

As the months crawled by, it soon became apparent just how much of a mess I was in. I was not under formal arrest, but rather under "preventative detention" on behalf of Canada. It certainly didn't feel like it. In truth, I felt like I had already been convicted. And despite my pleas to prison officials, I did not see a doctor once during my incarceration. Not an x-ray scan, not a blood test, not even an Aspirin: I was left to rot.

If it weren't for my knowledge as an oncologist, and the steady stream of chemotherapy drugs from trusted friends and colleagues, I would most certainly have died.

I decided, along with my lawyer, that waiting for due process would not be enough. We went public on our petition to the United Nations that my human rights were being violated. For this, I would receive yet more slings and arrows from the Canadian press, questioning why I did not simply give in to extradition and receive the treatment I needed. It did not seem to dawn on people that I still had rights. It was my prerogative to fight extradition and uphold my innocence. And because of what happened to my wife, who had been extradited a few months before, I did not have much confidence in the judicial process. I had my pride. Why should I play by their rules?

Along with the United Nations petition, we also put forth that Pamela had been forced to leave Panama without her consent.

I would not take the bait in Montreal. I would not be paraded around in a media spectacle, have my face splashed across the evening news, an ominous, slow-motion march to the courthouse set to music, as hordes of reporters stuck cameras and microphones in my face. I would have been cast as a villain, not as the embattled, cancer-stricken oncologist, former spy watchdog and ex-hospital-administrator returning home to defend himself. In the eyes of many people, I was guilty already. People even continued to doubt my illness, and the media did little to change this myth. I had every right to fight extradition.

My goal was simple: If I wasn't being charged, I wanted to be released on bond from La Joya Prison so I could receive cancer treatment in a proper hospital. From there, I would fight to return to the Bahamas so I might continue scheduled radiotherapy at the Cancer Centre, a place with excellent equipment and familiarity with my condition. And then I would invite Canadian authorities, once again, to come see me, on the record but without the press, so we could clear up these charges once and for all.

That plan proved to be a major challenge. There was much speculation over whether Canada had pressed Panama to keep me in prison. I do not doubt that Canada did little or nothing to help my cause, although a lot of the problem was simply the bureaucracy of La Joya. I learned that some inmates had been waiting years to even have a court date. The system was hopelessly, sometimes unbearably, slow.

I found ways to pass the time, and even to improve my circumstances and make everyday life tolerable. I had my cell—the space I shared with nine other inmates—carpeted. We all agreed on a rule where you had to take your shoes off before entering, or you had to wear "indoor" shoes. We became more respectful and acclimatized, creating rules about when you could make noise, and dividing up housekeeping responsibilities, such as who cleaned the toilet or fetched the rainwater. I had my "employees" do the chores for me.

I got to know my cellmates fairly well: a member of the Hells Angels from Quebec, one drug lord from the U.K. and another from Colombia, and two Jamaicans who had been caught carrying big payloads of narcotics. Normally, these inmates wouldn't secure a spot in a cell. I learned, however, that a place could be achieved through seniority, in terms of time spent. You can also buy your way in. Perhaps they had families that could provide that kind of money. Once you were in a cell, it was more or less permanent, unless you got out, were killed or decided to sell your spot.

While my life had become a bit more predictable, every once in a while something threw everything off balance. In July, a container ship known as the *Chong Chon Gang* left Cuba, bound for North Korea. The ship was navigating the Panama Canal when it was detained by authorities and searched. According to police, they discovered twenty-five containers of military hardware, including two Soviet-era MIG-21 fighter aircraft, air defense systems, missiles, and command and control vehicles. Word spread quickly in La Joya that the ship's crew, thirty-five North Koreans, were headed to prison.

Although I never saw the crew, their presence was felt immediately. Suddenly, communications within the prison became difficult. My lifeline to the outside world was unreliable at best as two governments exchanged demands and threats. More security was brought to the prison, and while there were no clashes, it changed our way of life.

One day around this time, a fellow inmate was found beheaded in one of the bathrooms. It was a statement killing, to be sure. These incidents happened, and I got used to them like someone watching a horror film on repeat until the blood and guts aren't scary anymore. I kept out of those affairs and stuck to what I do best: medicine.

As a doctor, I've got to know a lot about people. I would not go so far as to say I had friends. I had made acquaintances, some closer than others. Some people probably thought they were quite close to me. It is an approach I had used in the outside world as well, although it had become particularly important in La Joya, where relationships are simply a means for survival. The social structure of a prison is primeval, and it determined my associations. Because I was at the top of the pack, I could not befriend those below me. It was not for superficial reasons. It could be lethal to show too much sensitivity or openness. Order is achieved through fear and respect, and it is best to keep it that way.

Still, with ten men living in a cell's cramped quarters, I tried leaving the cell as often as possible, which was why I eventually invested in a "summer home." I use the term in jest, of course, but it was indeed exclusive in La Joya. On the roof, away from the seething hordes, I had a modest space. I shared it with three other people, but that is nothing by prison standards. We cooked food up there and got fresh air. It was a real privilege.

SIX MONTHS ON, I was the same Arthur Porter who went into La Joya. I was not a voyeur, sitting on the sidelines and just watching the game. I had entered the game, changed some rules and eventually moulded it to suit my needs. If there had been a vote in La Joya to nominate its leader, I would have had a shot.

However, I was more concerned with the outside world. My "summer home" on the roof was appreciated, but it only made my desire for freedom more acute. Salvation felt within my grasp. But I knew that forces at play in Canada

were making the situation difficult. Though I had been travelling on my diplomatic passport from Sierra Leone at the
time of my detainment, the embassy's high commissioner in
Washington later declared to the media that I did not have
any formal diplomatic status.

From what I understand, a great deal of pressure had
been placed on Sierra Leone to make that determina-
tion. There is no Sierra Leonean embassy in Ottawa, so it
is shared with the Americans in Washington. Heat from
Canadians might not have been enough to tip the scales,
but nobody wants to upset the Americans. Meanwhile, I
kept a letter from the president of Sierra Leone in my cell,
signed and authenticated, confirming my status as a goodwill ambassador.

Authorities placed screws on the Bahamas as well. My
contacts there informed me that government and financial
institutions had been pressured into disclosing my businesses and bank accounts, which they flatly refused to do.
For an offshore haven like the Bahamas, that would have
been reputational suicide.

Thinking back, the whole investigation felt sloppy from
the beginning. It was strange enough that I had to find out
about the charges through the media. I was never properly
served or contacted by Canadian authorities. My wife did
not even have the benefit of a media warning. She had to
find out about her charges while in transit, shortly before
being forcibly extradited to Canada.

I still believe it was a witch hunt. I was treated differently
from the beginning. It was about more than an alleged
white-collar crime in Montreal. It was about who I am, what
I have done, and most importantly, what I know.

I think some people in Ottawa, and certainly Quebec,

believe I have information that, if disclosed under oath, could be of significant embarrassment to the powers that be. At the end of the day, asking me about the hospital contract would involve probing the provincial government at the time. It was never Arthur Porter pronouncing an edict from up on high. There was an entire process, and it included many other people.

What a wonderful opportunity, perhaps, to have a field day with people who might be in the limelight today. The media would certainly love it. It would sell a lot of newspapers.

Who benefited from the scandal? The hospital did not. Quebec did not benefit either. snc-Lavalin, part of a much larger consortium, never stood to make much money from the contract. In the grand scheme of things, the mega-hospital would cost $1.3 billion, and they will probably make back only $1.3 billion. In other places, like Africa, it was possible to spend $200 million and make $1 billion. snc-Lavalin was interested in the hospital contract because it was on their home turf. I think it was probably encouraged to bid by the government of the day. This was its first hospital contract in Quebec, if not the world.

I believe there is interest in discrediting me in Quebec. The fact that I pulled through on that hospital was a black mark in many circles. And my various interests outside of McGill have made me a target too. Perhaps some resentment, jealousy or envy was in play to cut the tall poppy down. Meanwhile, the Conservative Party remained deathly quiet throughout my incarceration in La Joya. Given my political profile, they don't want to be dragged through the mud. I think many people hope I will never come back to Canada, under any circumstances.

It is a tangled web, and day by day I have tried to remain positive and unravel it.

IN OCTOBER, my lawyer received a letter, out of the blue, from the Canadian embassy in Panama, asking how I was doing and wondering if I needed anything. While Ricardo thanked them for asking about my well-being, he wrote:

> I have to state, however, my surprise that you have not advocated to have a terminal cancer sufferer, who is still under the presumption of innocence, placed under house arrest or the like. I am pleased that you have offered to help and clearly the most important items that my client needs on an urgent basis are a resupply of his life-saving chemotherapy and anticoagulation therapy.

For whatever reason, we never heard back. Were they simply paying lip service? Or did someone have a change of heart? I wish I knew.

Christmas and New Year's came and went. On December 25, I got dressed up in a grey suit and chequered rainbow bow tie. I strolled around the prison, taking photos. It was especially poignant for me because it was approximately one year since my original diagnosis. I was still here—and going strong.

From the beginning, I was determined to beat this, and with my new drugs, I remained optimistic. I continued making adjustments to my treatments. I developed a modest exercise routine and spent extra money to bring in vegetables to keep my strength and health in order. I still had a host of symptoms, of course. I had a bad cough and occasional shortness of breath, especially at night, requiring me to use the oxygen tank. At least twice a day I would have bouts of nausea, vomiting and diarrhea associated with my chemotherapy.

And then, in late February, I received some unexpected news. No, it was not help from the Canadian embassy. The prison staff informed me that on February 26, some eight months after I had been thrown in the hell hole, I would be taken to a hospital. True to their word, I was rushed out of the prison that morning with more security than the president. I had a convoy of five cars and four motorcycles, and a police helicopter circled overhead. I had to wear a bullet-proof vest and helmet. It was ridiculous. Four guards wearing ski masks and brandishing submachine guns sat with me in the car. Apparently they were worried that I might identify them. My former position with the Canadian security service, from what I understand, had the authorities in Panama spooked.

All the streets in town seemed closed off that morning. Speeding along, we did not encounter any traffic jams, and amid guns and security fanfare, they led me into the hospital and straight to a doctor's office. The result? I had a blood test. I was there for no more than ten minutes. Like the letter from the Canadian embassy, it all felt like a show, a farce.

I didn't feel confident about a follow-up appointment.

WHEN THE TIME comes, whether in La Joya or when I'm old and grey, I have a plot in Sierra Leone waiting for me. It's on a fantastic piece of land, beside other members of my family who have gone before. That is one thought, however, that I have tried not to dwell on.

It can sometimes seem easier to take a defeatist view. During my practice, I often saw black clouds drift across my patients' faces. Some of them started planning for their funerals shortly after leaving my office. I always got very anxious when this happened. I would take them away for a chat. I wanted my patients to fight and be committed to the process. At the same time, if you want to do something, do it now. Don't wait.

As for me, after my diagnosis I didn't want to vacation in Hawaii. I already lived in the Bahamas. I didn't want to climb Everest or Kilimanjaro. What I really wanted was to keep doing what I had always done—making something where there had been nothing, leaving something behind.

Wherever I have gone in life, something has survived me. In Detroit, when I was hired as CEO, we were losing millions upon millions of dollars. I had to cut the staff by seven thousand people right off the bat. Bankruptcy lawyers were literally in the room, but despite my critics, the Detroit Medical Center did not fold. And I took on the state and secured $150 million for the system's undesignated care.

In Sierra Leone, I introduced mining companies from all over the world, generating tens of millions of dollars in revenue and hundreds of new jobs. It brought structure and relative calm to a country that had been through one of the worst civil wars imaginable. We also built bridges, dams and other infrastructure. We had a Canadian company come in and build a school.

I did similar deals throughout Africa and the world. In my career of international business, I loved playing matchmaker, bringing together two parties and creating something new.

In the Caribbean, I helped launch the first cancer centre accredited by the American College of Oncology, and we would spread the institution's influence across the region, creating one big hospital separated only by water.

The McGill University Health Centre will perhaps always inspire question marks and conspiracy theories among Quebecers and other Canadians. The project took on a life of its own, to the point where it was rumoured that I was seven-foot-five and could shoot icicles out of my eyes. But above all the noise, that hospital will still be there. It will stand the test of time.

Through it all, I have had the privilege of knowing various heads of state, serving as their advisor and helping shape policy.

And then there were the patients, those countless souls who filed in and out of my office and received treatment. Some got better, others did not. But I never stopped fighting for them. I never stopped pushing. As an oncologist, I patented new techniques, built new centres, advised the World Health Organization, served on and established various boards and committees, and wrote more than three hundred research papers.

My patients didn't give up—and neither did I. Sitting in my jail cell, or milling around that prison, I viewed myself as someone who has been given great and unusual challenges. And I have never shrunk from them. I have taken on every obstacle—my own Mount Kilimanjaros—regardless of what stands in my path.

That, my dear reader, is how I want to be remembered.

EPILOGUE:
I KNOW WHO MY
FRIENDS ARE

WE STOOD AT the top of the stone steps leading down to the lawn and beach. The sun was shining, a slight breeze was in the air, and I could hear the distant notes of a string quartet.

I stared at the procession marching ahead, two by two, down the steps and out of view. Soon it would be our turn. My hand was shaking. Gemma squeezed it tightly, reassuringly. I felt her eyes upon me, but I couldn't meet her gaze.

It was a moment infused with conflicting emotions. I felt so happy, and so sad.

It was also a moment that I never thought I would live to see. It felt God-given. In the weeks and months leading up to my eldest daughter's wedding, another date had been spinning in my mind—the date cancer would overpower me. That date wasn't set in stone—and that was what made it so scary.

I didn't think I would make it. I had been diagnosed with lung cancer. Two weeks earlier, I was bedridden, reeling from the side effects of chemotherapy and radiotherapy. I was fighting, but not yet winning. I had been told my survival would be measured in months, that if I made it to the wedding I would need oxygen and a wheelchair. Instead, all I needed was a white hat with a grey brim to cover my chemo haircut. There I was, standing tall in a dark suit and purple bow tie, and never a prouder father than on that day.

I felt tears forming in my eyes, but I quickly brushed them aside with my other hand and took a deep breath. Ever since the diagnosis, I had never seen my children cry or get upset. I'm sure they had private moments. In my presence, though, my daughters always kept it together. They were strong for me; we all rallied together; and now I wanted to do the same for Gemma.

She squeezed my hand again and took a step forward. That was my cue. We linked arms and began our descent down the stone steps.

It was hard to not think about the uncertainty of the future. I was thankful for the moment, but I wanted more. After all, I wanted to one day walk my other three daughters down the aisle as well.

I worried that I wouldn't be there for Gemma and her future husband, Ryan Livingston. The two of them had known each other since high school in Michigan but had only started dating a few years ago. Pamela and I had always expected they would get married, although we never pushed it.

And then Ryan did the honourable thing. He arrived at our door in the Bahamas and asked us if he could ask Gemma to marry him.

So much had changed in just a few months. Our lives had been magical and somewhat of a fairy tale, I think. My wife and I were still in love after more than three decades of marriage. I had achieved a great deal in my professional life.

And we were parents to four wonderful girls. Meanwhile, we did not experience many of the problems other families faced. Perhaps that was why we were so united when adversity struck. We refused to accept hardship. We would analyze it, dissect it, defeat it and move on.

Our unity came from our differences. Not many families were like ours, with a father from Sierra Leone, a mother from the U.K. and lives lived in multiple countries. So we stuck together, whether we were physically in the same place or not. Distance never changed anything. No matter where I was in the world, or what I was doing, I spoke with all four of my daughters each and every day. When I was travelling the world for medical conferences or business, I always tried to take one of the girls with me, whether it was to China or to Spain. It was a bonding time. As adults, when we got together for Thanksgiving, birthdays or Christmas, we were intensely present, relishing the moment, because we knew it might be a long time before we were all together again.

When we found ourselves together at the dinner table, we would joke that the Internet was made for us. We adapted to new technology, personal websites, social networking and smart phones long before they were fashionable. They were not gimmicks, but rather essential tools of domestic communication when Dad worked in Canada, Mum lived in the Bahamas, Gemma lived in Michigan, Fiona and Adina were on either coast of Florida and Charlotte, the youngest, was at university in the U.K.

Pamela was the cornerstone, the anchor and our support. She used to tease me at times that she was a single parent, but it was always in jest. She set an incredible example for the children. We had different roles and carried them out well. Just how well would become evident when Pamela and

I were detained in Panama. "Team Porter," as I liked to call it, would spring into action, each of the girls dividing up responsibilities for my multinational business, communicating with various business partners, bankers, and even heads of state and making sure that life functioned well. All knew the meaning of family and would rise to the challenge.

But today, as we stepped off the stairs and onto the verdant lawn with the turquoise ocean beyond, I could see the upturned faces of my family and friends awaiting us. The string quartet's wedding march filled the air. Gemma and I walked breezily down the aisle between the chairs set up on the lawn, towards the canopy and her husband-to-be.

I sat down in the front row beside Pamela. Her eyes were wide and shining. I looked at Gemma and Ryan and listened as they exchanged their vows. I couldn't help but glance behind me as well, at our friends from several countries, collected over a lifetime. I might have ten thousand names in my address book, but only twenty or so are friends. My friendships have all sprouted from my career, because that was where I spent the vast majority of my time.

My eyes first drifted to Karol Sikora, one of my oldest friends, and his wife, Alison. Karol had just become a junior consultant in oncology at Cambridge University when I first entered his life. Having just finished medical school, I became his first intern for a period of six months. And we had remained close ever since. Small in stature but big in brainpower and spirit, he was the author of *Cancer*, a large tome nearly equal to his body weight. It became a standard reference book for oncologists, and indeed it is just one of twenty or so books he has authored or co-authored in his career.

Karol was fearless. The son of a military officer in the Free Polish Air Force and a Scottish mother, he took on controversial issues with gusto. He battled on behalf of patients with the British government and remained critical of the National Health Service, saying things that were true but generally were never said. Why did some patients get better care than others? Why did some get their needed drugs and others didn't? Karol was certainly part of the "establishment." He was a member of the Athenaeum Club in central London, a place that held as members many of the Nobel laureates that Britain has produced over the last century. But he was not afraid to be unpopular and fight the status quo.

Karol was the brain behind Cancer Partners UK, a start-up company developing small "doc in a box" cancer centres across the U.K. to ensure the highest standards of care to the population without the spectre of government rationing.

He also achieved international notoriety because of his association with convicted Lockerbie bomber Abdelbaset al-Megrahi. Karol was instrumental in al-Megrahi's compassionate release from a Scottish jail in 2009, more than twenty years after the infamous Pan Am Flight 103 exploded over Lockerbie on its way to New York City. Karol's report concluded that al-Megrahi suffered from terminal prostate cancer and only had months to live.

Karol was a maverick. He enjoyed taking risks, which is probably why we got along so well. I wanted to see what was on the other side of the fence. Not only that, I wanted to question why the fence was there in the first place. I gravitated to people who asked hard questions.

Don Ragan, my maverick physicist, was sitting a few rows down from Karol. I first met him in Detroit, and he was my right-hand man in ensuring that what our expensive linear accelerators delivered, in terms of dose, was what the physicians planned to give. I also respected him because he could turn his hand to everything from sailing to flying. He taught himself to sail by going out and coming back. Fortunately, before going up in a plane, he took a few lessons. But I can guarantee he took as few as possible. He knew when to use the manual and when to throw it away.

In the Woodstock era, he lived in a commune, and met his wife there. We often saw each other in the Bahamas. Rather than buy a house there, he settled on a sixty-foot boat in the harbour.

Then I locked eyes with Conville Brown, my Bahamian business partner and friend. A noted cardiologist and savvy entrepreneur, he first met me over the telephone when he sent a patient with prostate cancer to Detroit for treatment. Although an ocean separated us, we clicked that day, and it wasn't long before we were in deep conversation at my house. We were very similar—loved a challenge, loved an opportunity and loved to succeed. The day we met, we both knew instinctively that we would be business partners. Soon the Cancer Centre Bahamas was born. It became the leading centre in the region, with connections in Turks and Caicos, Antigua and Barbuda, Trinidad and Tobago, and the Eastern Caribbean.

Many people have been in and out of my life; a handful of enemies, a great deal of "frenemies." And just a few close friends.

When I think about the people with whom I have worked, the right-hand men and close colleagues with whom I spent countless hours over the years, it dawns on me that I barely knew them at all. I was never invited to their homes for dinner or a drink. I never met their children. I tended to avoid socializing with professional colleagues, and that could be very isolating.

Many people have schools, sporting events, volunteer groups, churches, mosques or synagogues as meeting places, serving as fertile ground for friendships. I had none or very few of those things. The boardroom was my environment, and only particular things grow there. I suppose my ambition in medicine, business and politics bred loneliness, even isolation, wherever I roamed. And my life was so often scrutinized and placed under a microscope that it caused me to withdraw even further into myself.

I have always been proud of my accomplishments, but part of me wishes that I had stopped more often to smell the flowers.

It was interesting to see which friends stayed and which fled when things got difficult. Many people purported to be my close friends and colleagues. They performed all the little pleasantries that friends do, and weren't bashful about sucking on the teat when it suited them, as my career grew and prospered. But once the chips were down, I heard every excuse in the book. My job won't allow it. I don't want my boss knowing we're friends. I've just been so busy lately.

A few people surprised me, in terms of how quickly they disappeared. For the most part, however, I think we all know who our friends are. Perhaps, in the hustle and blur of everyday life, we don't always see them clearly or appreciate them. But the ones I expected to run, ran. The ones I knew would stay, stayed. It affirmed my faith in humanity.

As Gemma and Ryan spoke their vows by the sea, and sealed them with a kiss, we cheered and took photos. Suddenly, my diagnosis and legal problems no longer mattered. Surrounded by my loved ones, I felt nothing but gratitude for everyone in my life.

The world is full of fair-weather friends. I know who my real friends are now.

INDEX